RIDGES and VALLEYS III

A Third Collection of Walks in the Midlands

by

Trevor Antill

Meridian Books

Published 1994 by Meridian Books

© Trevor Antill 1994

ISBN 1-869922-22-0

A catalogue record for this book is available from the British Library.

The right of Trevor Antill to be identified as the author of this work has been asserted by him in accordance with the Copyright, Designs and Patents Act 1988.

All rights reserved. No part of this publication may be copied, reproduced or transmitted in any form or by any means without the prior written permission of the publishers.

> **Publishers' Note**
> Every care has been taken in the preparation of this book. All the walks have been independently checked and are believed to be correct at the time of publication. However, neither the author nor the publishers can accept responsibility for any errors or omissions or for any loss, damage, injury or inconvenience resulting from the use of the book. Please remember that the countryside is continually changing: hedges and fences may be removed or re-sited; landmarks may disappear; footpaths may be re-routed or be ploughed over and not reinstated (as the law requires); concessionary paths may be closed. The publishers would be very pleased to have details of any such changes that are observed by readers.

Maps based upon the Ordnance Survey maps with the permission of the Controller of Her Majesty's Stationery Office. © Crown Copyright.

Meridian Books
40 Hadzor Road, Oldbury, Warley, West Midlands B68 9LA

Printed in Great Britain by BPC Wheatons Ltd., Exeter.

Contents

Introduction		iv
Location Map		v
Transport		vi
1	Erratic Legends	1
	Clent Hills – 5 miles	
2	Come Blow Your Horn	4
	Enville – 5½ miles	
3	A Brewers Gift	9
	Barlaston – 5¾ miles	
4	By River and Rail	13
	Bridgnorth – 6½ miles	
5	By Eckington!	17
	Great Comberton – 6½ miles	
6	The Suckley Hills	21
	Lulsley – 7 miles	
7	Riding the Range	27
	Cannock Chase – 7½ miles	
8	A Walk that has the Edge	30
	Brown Edge – 7¾ miles	
9	Border Town	37
	Kinver – 8½ miles	
10	Iron Age to Iron Horse	42
	Craven Arms – 9½ miles	
11	England's Kitchen Garden	48
	Little Witley – 9½ miles, 6 miles, 5¼ miles	
12	A Contrasting Circuit	57
	The Malverns – 9¾ miles	
13	A Midland Magnet	64
	Bridgnorth – 10 miles	
14	Faith, Hope and a Little Charity	70
	Hope Bowdler – 10¼ miles, 5½ miles, 4¾ miles	
15	On Ditchford Bank	76
	Hanbury – 10½ miles	
16	Diddlebury Delights	82
	Diddlebury – 11 miles	
17	Banners for the Buzzards	88
	Craven Arms – 14 miles, 7 miles, 7 miles	
18	Severn Leagues	95
	Wolverley – 21 miles	
Index		105

Introduction

This third book of walks, following the Ridges and Valleys theme, remains within the three Midland counties of Shropshire, Staffordshire and Worcestershire. Again the selected walks explore some of the lesser known parts of those counties as well as some of the better known. All contain a local or historic dimension to add to the enjoyment of this special part of England.

As I have mentioned in previous books our countryside is constantly and frequently changing which may lead to the occasional difference between text and terrain. It is recommended that the appropriate map and a compass are carried. As an aid to navigation across large fields and in poor visibility, compass bearings are sometimes used in the text: remember, all bearings quoted are Grid North rather than Magnetic North.

The seasons also have a significance to any country walk. In summer, shorts and sandals should; in my view; be confined to the beach: with few exceptions the English countryside is not the place for such disportment! Our climate is one that provides an ideal breeding ground for things like nettles, brambles and insects and as a result such flimsy clothing is definitely not 'user friendly'. Conversely, our winter climate helps to make Britain that green and pleasant land so beloved of the romantic poets – in other words, it rains a lot! Consequently mud and water may be encountered and the appropriate equipment should therefore be utilised; gaiters can be a great boon. Remember, if it's in your rucksack you can wear it – if it ain't, you cain't!

Again all Rights of Way have been checked to the Definitive Maps and all the route descriptions have been independently checked. For their willing and patient help especial thanks are due to the Rights of Way staffs at Shropshire, Staffordshire and Hereford & Worcester County Councils. For checking the routes I am once again grateful to Barbara Bunney, Rex Evans, John Greatbatch, Peter Groves, Tony Limb, Sheila & Albert Purcell, Ken Unwin and Arthur Welch.

As I anticipate moving on to a new theme, I rather doubt that there will be any more books in the Ridges and Valleys series – quit while you're ahead they say! Nonetheless I hope your appetites have been sufficiently whetted to find many more of your own ridges and valleys. I wish you good luck, good weather and good walking.

Trevor Antill

'Take time while time is, for the time will away'. (Old English Proverb)

Also by the author:
Ridges and Valleys: Walks in the Midlands
Ridges and Valleys II: More Walks in the Midlands
The Navigation Way: A hundred mile towpath walk (second edition) (with Peter Groves)

Location Map

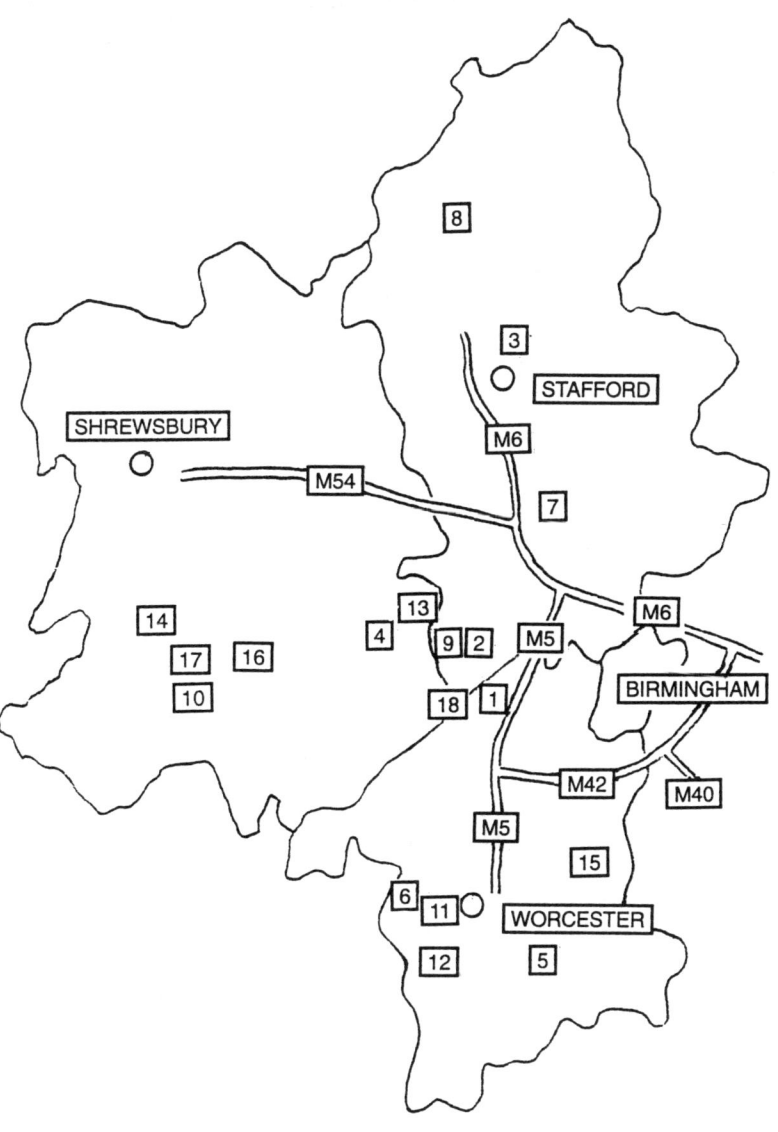

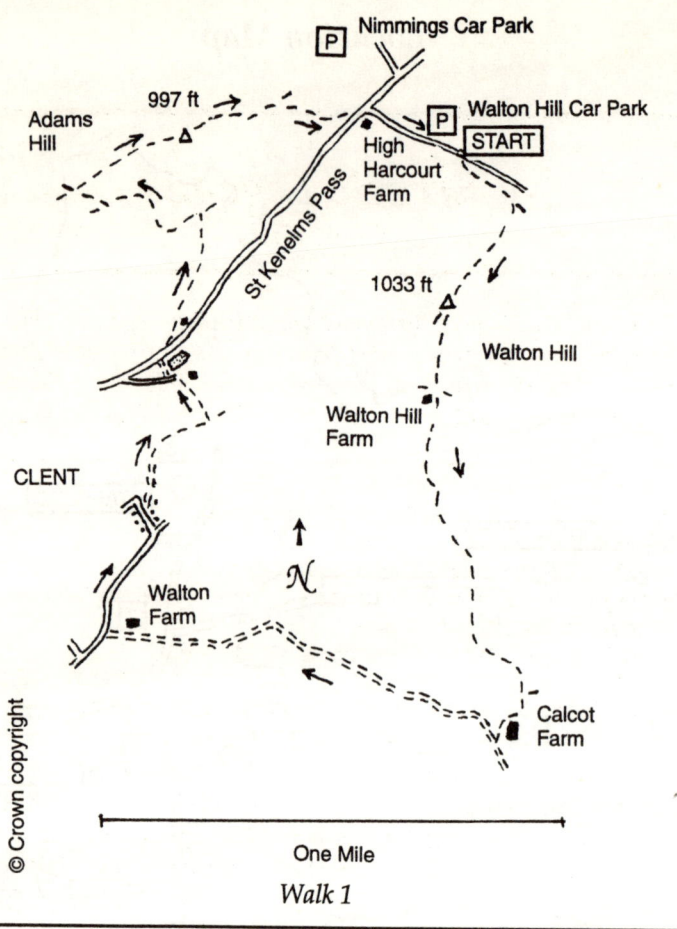

Walk 1

Transport

All the walks in this book are circular and should present no problems of access to motorists. Also, a number can be reached by public transport, although in a few cases this involves some extra walking. Details are given in the introductory boxes to each walk. Because of the variability of services you should always check on times before setting out. Some useful telephone numbers are:

British Rail (Birmingham): 021-643 2711
Bus Services: Hereford & Worcester, 0905-766800;
                Shropshire, 0345-056 785;
                Staffordshire, 0785-223344;
                West Midlands, 021-200 2700

1
Erratic Legends
Clent Hills

The Clent Hills and their surrounds are steeped in legend. While some are authoritative and well documented others are, to say the least, imaginative. Nonetheless they add a fascinating – and at times amusing – dimension to an outstanding hill walk that largely falls within National Trust land.

> DISTANCE: 5 miles
> MAPS: Landranger (1:50,000) 139. Pathfinder (1:25,000) 933 & 953
> PARKING: Walton Hill car parks
> PUBLIC TRANSPORT: Midland Red West services 192/292/193. Alight for Hagley Wood Lane. Walk up the lane, turn right at the T-junction, then left to reach Walton Hill car park.
> START/FINISH: Walton Hill car parks (GR 943803)

FROM the enclosed Walton Hill car park follow the railed path – signed North Worcestershire Path (NWP) – that starts left of a notice board. As you rise you will shortly meet railed steps left and right. Go right up this crossing path to gain the lower crest of Walton Hill where you go forward to follow the ridge upwards to a triangulation pillar at 1033 feet.

It is maintained that Walton Hill was the scene of a battle between Britons and Romans when, on this occasion, the Romans where driven down the hill and defeated. However there is some doubt about this for nearby Wychbury Hill is also regarded as a possible site for the battle and in addition a nineteenth century account of the Walton Hill conflict places it some decades after the Romans left Britain!

At the pillar the track splits. Follow the left fork and in a few yards pass a NWP post to continue with the bridleway and arrive in front of a house at a junction of tracks. Here go left to quickly pass through a vehicle barrier and join the track to the house. Immediately opposite is a fence stile (NWP) that you cross to go forward along the clear path left of the garden. Cross another fence stile and continue forward at the top of an embankment with a hedge on your right.

Continue following this well trodden terrace path and NWP marker posts until your path descends to meet a track coming up from the left. Merging with the track continue forward with the fence to your right. In a short while your footpath (NWP) branches off left from the track to pick up another fence on the right. In a while, after passing under power lines, you will come to a fence stile next to a gate.

Over this the NWP route goes immediately left and down to another stile. Do not follow it however, instead...

Cross over the fence stile and continue straight ahead on a clear path keeping the hedge and fence on your right. In a few yards, and before a barn conversion, you will arrive at a broad step stile – marked 'Footpath' – on your right and in the fence. Go over the stile and forward with the barbed wire fence to its protruding corner where a public footpath signpost directs you left and down to a step stile in the bottom corner. To your left is the large house at Calcot Farm. Cross the step stile into a fenced and hedged green lane.

The Glacial Boulder

As you cross the step stile immediately on the left of it is an erratic – a rock that does not naturally belong to the surrounding area. This particular block of granite was transported from the Arennig mountains in North Wales by the Welsh ice sheet in the glacial period.

Ahead of you is a wind pump and in the field (at the time of writing) a herd of fallow deer.

In the green lane turn right and simply follow it for about a mile to arrive at Walton Farm and a T-junction with a surfaced lane.

Turn right to follow the lane uphill. Just after the Foresters Nursing Home there is a 'No Through Road' sign and a road name-sign for Highfield Lane. At this junction take the left and lower lane to pass left of the white cottages – note the iron water pump and horse collar. After a short slope in the lane you will come to a sign – 'Walton Rise' – with a Clent Parish Council notice board next to it.

Here go right and up to leave the tarmac behind and pass two trees bearing signs 'No

Unauthorised Parking' and 'No Parking'. Soon reaching a gate, step stile and blue bridleway arrow cross over to continue following your broad track. In a few yards, at a junction of tracks, go right to pass a National Trust sign. Keeping the fence on your right, a little further on you will come to a marker post at a junction of tracks. Take the left, lower bridleway to descend fairly steeply to upright vehicle barrier posts near a house. Go through the posts onto the drive in front of the house to then go left and down to meet the gates of Moors Cottage. Here go left again, along the tarmac, for about 30 yards where on the right, next to a white gate, you will find an enclosed footpath. Turn right into the footpath and follow it past a pool to shortly meet a road.

Go right along the road for another 30 yards where on the left you will see an unsigned sandy path, next to a short section of wooden fencing, ascending an embankment. Join this path and follow it up to pass left of 'Danes Dyke' and so through a few trees to reach the open hillside. Although there are many paths and tracks going off in different directions you follow your main path as it steadily rises to meet a broad, crossing bridle track – to the right is a stand of trees.

Here, joining the broad track, go left and follow it as it generally contours the hillside. In a while it gently rises to a small crest where there is a junction of paths. *To the left is a vehicle barrier at the edge of conifer trees while just a few yards to the right is a bench seat.* Go forward for about 10 yards where your bridleway splits again. Take the right-hand upper track which shortly brings you to the sloping main ridge of Adams Hill. Here go right and up the broad ridge to an isolated stand of trees.

Near the trees are the four standing stones erected in the eighteenth century to supposedly enhance the view. Next to these is a triangulation pillar at 997 feet while on the other side there is a toposcope. A little further away is an observation platform with graphics identifying the surrounding landscape. Certainly the summit is a popular and long ranging vantage point with good views through 360 degrees.

From the triangulation pillar continue forward along the broad ridge – you are now back on the North Worcestershire Path. In a shallow dip take the waymarked track (NWP) on the right and start descending the hillside. This bridleway will bring you down to the surfaced road at St. Kenelm's Pass.

Kenelm was the ninth century boy-king of Mercia who succeeded his father at the tender age of seven. He had an adult sister who coveted power and persuaded her lover – the boy's guardian – to take him hunting and kill him. This he did burying the body where the twelfth century church now stands. Later the body was found and a spring is reputed to have started flowing at the spot. Subsequently a shrine was built on the site and Kenelm was canonised: later a church was built on the site of the shrine. It is said the spring existed until the reign of Henry VIII! St.Kenelm's church is about half a mile left along the surfaced road.

Go left along the surfaced road and shortly right along the road signed for 'Walton Hill'. This quickly brings you back to the car park.

2
Come Blow Your Horn
Enville

The far south-west corner of Staffordshire contains a special area for those who like to walk. Centred on Enville, essentially an estate village, and contained within the estates of Enville Hall; the Sheepwalks are a fascinating blend of high rolling pasture, mixed woodland and attractive pools. Though only 675 feet at their highest, they offer superb views in virtually every direction. As the crow flies they are some four miles from the edge of Stourbridge and are therefore, not surprisingly, very popular with the more discerning walker.

Though parking can be difficult in Enville village – see the off-road parking elsewhere on this route – it is the natural point from which to start this most enjoyable of walks.

Meals are available at the Cat Inn; except on Sundays!

DISTANCE: 5½ miles
MAPS: Landranger (1:50,000) 138. Pathfinder (1:25,000) 933
PARKING: Limited in Enville village. Off-road on the A458 near Newhouse Farm (GR 809872) on a minor road at GR 812883 and also where the Staffordshire Way crosses another minor road (GR 820875)
START/FINISH: The Cat Inn, Enville (GR 826868)

IN ENVILLE village walk along the drive between the Cat Inn and the enclosed 'village green'. Passing through a white gate follow the drive to pass the cricket ground on the left and soon arrive at the old stable block in front of Enville Hall.

Enville Hall is the home of the Grey family, Earls of Stamford, and dates mostly from the eighteenth century. In 1904 the Hall was badly damaged by fire following which the interior was largely renewed. The surrounding hills, woodlands and watercourses were utilised by that well known poet and landscaper, William Shenstone of Halesowen, who largely created the parkland you are about to enjoy. His landscaping seems to have endured more than his poetry!

The Cat Inn is one of the few public houses in England that 'enjoys' a six day licence, it being closed on Sundays. This unusual fact dates from the last century when a restrictive covenant – the freehold landlord being the estate – was included in the lease.

Just past the stable block there is a large gateway with ornamental gates and lamps atop the pillars where, just a few yards beyond the gateway and

Come Blow Your Horn 5

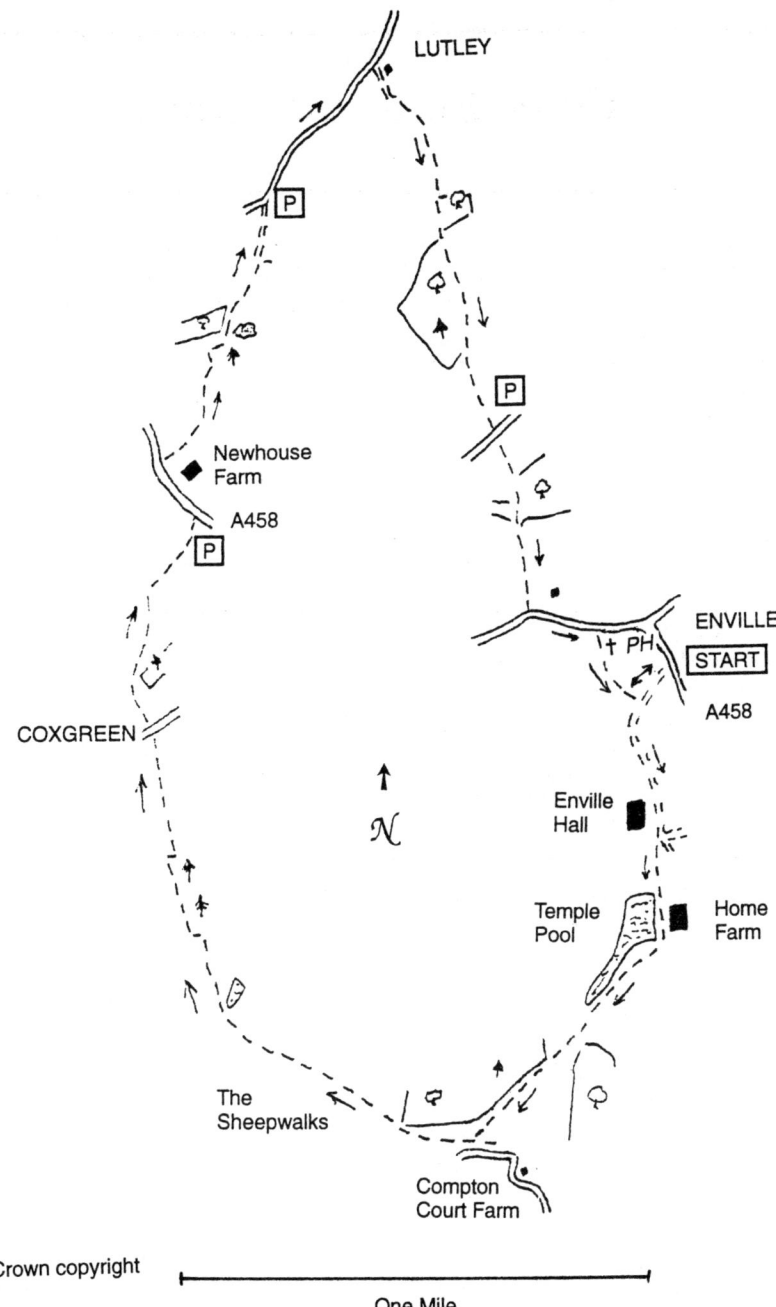

at the end of the wall, there is a step stile. Cross this and walk directly across the pasture aiming for the right hand edge of the Home Farm outbuildings.

This line brings you to another step stile next to an old wrought iron gate. Go over to follow the clear track between the farm buildings and Temple Pool where you quickly cross two gated step stiles. After the second swing half right to follow a grassy track, walking roughly parallel to the 'tail' of the pool, and pass through a gate to continue up to another which has a step stile a few yards to the left of it. From here go half left, up the slope, to the corner of trees where you now continue forward with the woodland edge on your right. Just before reaching the top right corner of this steep pasture, where there is a gate, leave the woodland fence by going slightly left to a marker post next to a waymarked step stile and gate.

Over the step stile now walk up, slightly right, to the trees again where there is a marker post. *Your way across the Sheepwalks is now shown by frequent use of these marker posts.* Joining the metal fence around the trees follow it forward to the protruding corner where you leave it to walk ahead to the right hand corner of a short section of fencing around young trees. Here you follow the same line, with the fence on your left, to shortly leave it at the next corner to reach another marker post. This now directs you upwards again towards the brow of the pastures, aiming for the left of a fence surrounding trees. At this point the pasture falls away quite steeply.

On this last described section you will have enjoyed stunning views in most directions, probably the best in South Staffordshire. Now you will see, ahead and in the distance, the Clee and Malvern Hills.

After taking in these views start to make your way down the slope following the marker posts to the left edge of a pool where there is a step stile. Cross into a field and immediately turn right for the few yards to its corner. Here go left up the field edge with the hedge on your right to then descend to the bottom corner just in front of a stand of conifers. Here a marker post directs you a short distance left to a hedge gap next to an oak tree. Go right through the gap, into a field, and then immediately right to the corner next to the conifer plantation. In the corner turn left to follow the field edge and the plantation to the next corner where there is another marker post directing you right along a hedged and sunken path. As you come to the end of the hedged section of the path you will see, on the left, a step stile in a short section of wooden fencing. Cross this stile into the field where you go directly forward across the field to a gateway and a culverted ditch. To the left you can see the half timbered farmhouse of Coxgreen Farm. Again continue forward into the next field and follow the left hand hedge up to the road at Coxgreen.

At the road cross over to the field gate opposite, left of the cottage, and enter the field. Walk forward with the right hand hedge to its protruding corner where you leave it to go very slightly right, aiming for the left corner of woodland. Meeting the fence around the woodland, and then immediately leaving it, follow the same line for the short distance to the protruding corner of the left hand hedge. Here go straight ahead again, so cutting the inverted corner, to a waymarked step stile in another corner. Crossing this double step stile go right to immediately pass through a gateway where you have fields left and right. Enter the left hand field and continue forward to follow the right hand hedge towards a large oak tree. There is a yellow waymark arrow on the oak tree! Continue to follow this field edge until reaching the A458.

At the A458 turn left and follow it as it bends to pass Newhouse Farm on the right and a public footpath sign on the left. Immediately past the black and white timbered 'Chadthorne' cottage you will arrive at a public footpath sign and step stile, also on the right.

Crossing the step stile into a field go diagonally left to the far left corner where there is a step stile next to a wooden power pole. Go over into a large field and straight across it to the far hedge and a waymarked oak tree (approx. 45 degrees). Arriving at the oak tree go left for 25 yards where on a protruding corner there is a step stile in the hedge. Cross into the next field to go immediately left and follow the left hedge down to the corner and another step stile. Go over this into the next field and, still with the left hedge, follow it to a point just before the next corner where there is a step stile on your left next to a large oak tree.

Climbing the stile into scrub trees, immediately before more dense woodland, swing right onto a track to follow a line of poplars. This will bring you to pass immediately left of a stand of conifers where you continue with the track along the edge of the conifers to a pool. Immediately before the pool the track swings left and you follow it to soon reach a gate and waymarked step stile. Here continue straight ahead into a hedged green lane and follow it forward to meet a minor road.

Follow the road right for about a third of a mile, passing a pool on the way, until reaching the first house on the right at Lutley. Here there is a public footpath sign pointing right along a hedged track at the side of the house. Following it, you have now joined the Staffordshire Way, will bring you to a gate and step stile. Entering a field go forward and left, with the left hedge, to the next corner where there is a Staffs Way signpost between a stile and a gate. Ignore both the stile and the gate to follow the direction of the sign right along the bottom edge of the field to a step stile under a large oak tree in the next corner. Cross into the next field and continue on the same line, with the hedge and ditch on your left, to arrive at the bottom corner where you descend to a wooden hunters' gate and footbridge. On the other side follow the clear path through a few trees to a step stile into a field. Over this stile go forward along the edge heading for wooden fencing where in a few yards you will pass a Staffs Way sign. In the wooden fencing are two step stiles that you ignore. Instead keep the fencing on your right and follow it up around the edge of the field to join a woodland edge. Follow the woodland – on your right – up to another step stile that you cross into another field and so continue forward with the woodland fence and a pool on your right. In the next corner cross another step stile and follow the woodland to its end where you join a hedge to follow that forward also keeping it on your right. Ignore and pass a stile in the hedge to follow it up to a tarmac lane.

Cross the lane to the step stile opposite and follow the field edge down to the bottom corner where you cross a waymarked step stile and then a footbridge. On the other side you pass through an old wooden gate at a Staffs Way sign where you swing left to follow the field edge to a pair of step stiles. Crossing both go forward on a hedged and slightly sunken path to reach a white metal gate that takes you onto the edge of a large lawn. Keeping right, follow the right hand fence and walk up past the large house to reach the A458.

At the road go left as far as Enville church where you turn right into its car park.

Standing on a prominent rise above the village and Hall, this Church of St. Mary stands on Norman foundations but was extensively restored by Sir Gilbert Scott, in the style of Gloucester Cathedral, during the late nineteenth century.

Entering the churchyard pass in front of the tower and under the inevitable yew tree to the bottom wall where there is a step stile into a field. In the field go half left (135 degrees) aiming for the wooden shed at the end of a garden. As you get nearer the shed you will see a gate and step stile that you cross into a wide fenced track. Follow the track for a short distance where you join the main drive to Enville Hall. Now turn left along the drive back to the Cat Inn

Blackberry

3
A Brewers Gift
Barlaston

Just a cursory glance at the relevant map might persuade you to dismiss this southern edge of the Potteries: to do so would mean missing an outstanding ridge and valley walk.

A large part of this circular walk explores Downs Banks, an expanse of heathland in the care of the National Trust. While it is close to Meaford Power Station in the upper Trent Valley – where river, rail, road and canal all funnel through a narrow gap – and not far from the Potteries themselves; none of these features intrude into this happy oasis which offers splendid views from choice vantage points.

The walk also takes in the attractive village of Barlaston which hosts the Wedgwood Visitor Centre.

> DISTANCE: 5¾ miles
> MAPS: Landranger (1:50,000) 127. Pathfinder (1:25,000) 830
> PARKING: Ford and lay-by at edge of Downs Banks (GR 899363) and the nearby National Trust car park (GR 900366)
> PUBLIC TRANSPORT: British Rail to Barlaston. Leave the station and follow the road east for about a third of a mile to the village green and cenotaph. Now follow the directions at ➡ on page 12
> START/FINISH: The road and ford at the edge of Downs Banks (GR 899363)

TO START a walk by leaving a National Trust boundary behind you might seem unusual; nonetheless this is precisely what you do, for your initial circle, in an area of close contours, gives a good introduction to this compact part of Staffordshire.

Leaving the ford behind you, and walking south along the road, soon pass Brook Cottage on the left and in just a few yards meet a lane junction; also on the left. Go left along the lane and in about 100 yards; on the left and immediately after a telegraph pole; you will see a step stile. Crossing over into a field now walk across its centre, aiming for a poplar tree to the right of the bungalow on the crest of the second field. Following this line will bring you to two gates in the opposite hedge where there is a step stile. Cross into the second field and walk up the embankment to the poplar tree. At the tree go forward to a fence bordering the drive that leads to the bungalow. At the fence go right and follow it to the corner of the field. Just before the corner there is an old gate in the fence and next to it the remains of a rotting step stile. Cross the stile onto the drive of 'The Quails' – the bungalow – and go right to follow it through gates onto a tarmac lane.

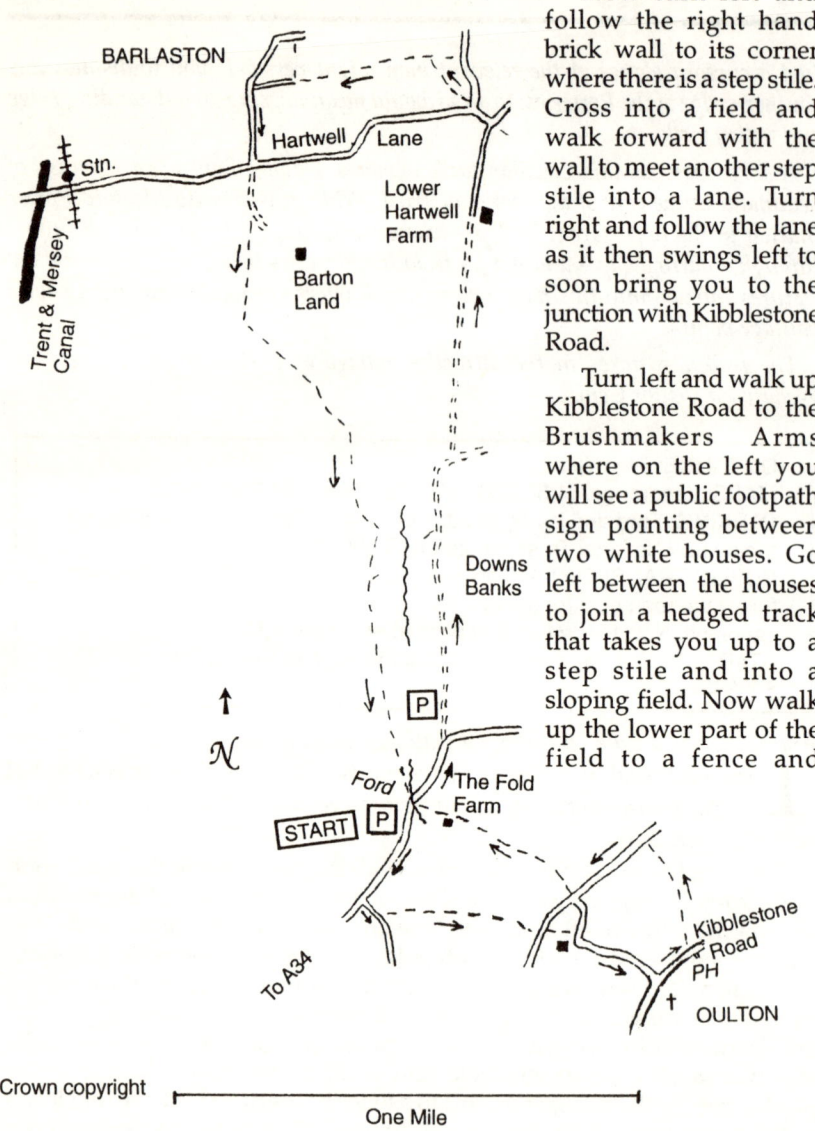

Now turn left and follow the right hand brick wall to its corner where there is a step stile. Cross into a field and walk forward with the wall to meet another step stile into a lane. Turn right and follow the lane as it then swings left to soon bring you to the junction with Kibblestone Road.

Turn left and walk up Kibblestone Road to the Brushmakers Arms where on the left you will see a public footpath sign pointing between two white houses. Go left between the houses to join a hedged track that takes you up to a step stile and into a sloping field. Now walk up the lower part of the field to a fence and another step stile. Over the stile go a little right to pick up a line of stunted trees – mostly crab apple – and follow them up to a finger post and step stile onto a metalled lane.

In the lane go left and down the hill until arriving at the entrance to Midfield Nurseries. Turn right through the nursery gates and follow the tarmac forward to its end. Here continue on the same line to pass between hedges and arrive at a line of Leyland cypress trees near to their left edge. At a gap in the trees you will see an unusual fence stile that takes you into a field. Now follow the left fence forward and down to a gate and step stile into another field. *Ahead and across the valley can be seen the heathland on Downs Banks.* Now on a track follow the same line down to a corner with another gate and step stile. In the next field maintain your line to the bottom left corner where there is a gate and step stile in front of a house. Cross the stile and walk between the house and its garage to join the drive down to a tarmac lane. Immediately to your left is the ford from which you started.

Turn right along the lane and follow it until arriving at the gateway and unsurfaced road on the left that gives entry into Downs Banks. Go left along it to the National Trust car park.

The Downs consist of 160 acres of heathland and were once planted with hops for use in the nearby Joule's brewery. Demonstrating a commendable public spirit – no pun intended – the brewery purchased this beauty spot so as to prevent its fall into industrial use for the nearby Meaford Power Station. The Downs are crossed by a trackway traditionally regarded as part of the ancient packhorse route from Chester to the East Midlands.

Near the car park there is a commemorative granite block inscribed 'These Downs were purchased by John Joule & Sons Ltd, endowed by public subscription, and presented to the National Trust on 22 July 1950 as a thank offering for victory in the war of 1939-45 and as a memorial to those who fell in the war'

Follow the unsurfaced road past the car park and through a vehicle barrier where it reduces to a track. *As might be expected in an area of open access there are many paths and bridleways that radiate off this main track.* Your route is to stay on the main track; keeping the valley bottom and stream to your left; as it meticulously progresses forward and northward. As you approach the end of the heathland the track starts to rise and then swings right to a gate leading you out of the National Trust land. Go through the gate and at a junction of tracks, when adjacent to a National Trust sign, turn left into a broad fenced track. Follow this down when it narrows to a nice hedged bridleway and then arrives at a gate just before Lower Hartwell Farm. Go through the gate and pass in front of the farmhouse to join the tarmac lane that continues forward. In a little while reach Hartwell Lane at a bend.

Turn left along Hartwell Lane and in a few yards go right into a joining lane. In about 20 yards you will see a rickety fence stile and footpath sign on the left. Cross into the field and walk forward to follow the left hand hedge under the overhead cables. Just before the end of the field you will see to the left a gate and step stile where the ditch has been culverted. Cross into the neighbouring field and walk forward now with a hedge on your right. In a short distance and near a concrete water trough you will arrive at two close stiles, one in the crossing fence in front and one in the hedge right. Ignoring the right hand stile cross the one in front and continue forward, still with the hedge on your right, to the next field corner. Here, next to a gate, you will find a substantial two-step stile that you cross. Now in a cricket field continue the same line along the edge with the hedge now on your left. Passing in front of the pavilion turn immediately left to a kissing gate in the field corner. Through the kissing gate 'The Grange' courtyard is in front of you. Turn right and follow the tarmac lane to a T-junction where you now turn left towards the centre of Barlaston.

➡ Arriving at the village green, cenotaph and cross-roads; cross over to follow the minor road opposite (turn right if walking from the railway station) which is signed for 'The Barton Land Home' – it also has a public footpath sign at its entrance. Follow it to pass a private car park and walk through a white gateway where in just a few yards you will come to an ornamental iron gate. To the right of this gate is a public footpath sign and a kissing gate that you go through.

Now following the bottom edge of parkland, with a fence on your right, walk to the next corner where there is another wooden kissing gate. Through this go forward and slightly left on a clear path aiming for the top left edge of trees in the distance. Passing through a gap stile at the side of a gate follow the embanked track up to the woodland where it passes between gates and fences to a step stile. Crossing the stile takes you back onto Downs Banks where you walk forward with the right hand fence to pass a National Trust sign. Here follows a superb ridge walk with good views. Now all you need to do is stay at the top of the ridge, following the right hand fence, until after a while it takes you down on a clear path to the stream in the valley bottom. At the stream turn right to follow it to a gap stile in the boundary fence and so onto your lay-by.

Emperor dragonfly

4
By River and Rail
Bridgnorth

Divided between High Town and Low Town, Bridgnorth is a historic market town connected by the steepest Cliff Railway in the country. Standing on a sandstone ridge the leaning Norman keep occupies a commanding position overlooking this ancient river crossing. High Town in particular offers many historic buildings while below it the Severn Valley Railway provides a nostalgic reminder of more recent bygone times.

The higher parts of the walk offer panoramic views across the Severn Valley and into Shropshire.

DISTANCE: 6½ miles
MAPS: Landranger (1:50,000) 138
Pathfinder (1:25,000) 911
PARKING: Public Car Parks in Bridgnorth
PUBLIC TRANSPORT: Buses: Midland Red North service 890 from Wolverhampton. Trains: Severn Valley Railway (when operating) from Kidderminster.
START/FINISH: Severn Valley Railway, Bridgnorth. (GR 715929)

FROM the Severn Valley Railway station pass the first car park, and the Hollyhead Inn, to a second sign for SVR parking. Here there is a left turn – Station Street – which you follow to bear left again along the side of various industrial units. Soon reaching a large, new, brick, engine shed turn right with a footpath sign along the path that rises between gardens and the tarmac track leading to the overflow car park. Arriving at a stile cross it to enter school playing fields.

Walking forward on the same line reach the end of gardens and follow them to the corner of the playing fields where a stile awaits you. Cross it and follow the path as it swings right to meet and cross the footbridge over the new bypass. On the other side go left to a stile and so right over it into a field. Taking the right hand of two paths follow the right hedge and aim for the small church steeple ahead. Ignoring a stile in the hedge, carry on to the field corner and cross another stile to reach the small car park at the church and so join the B4363. Here a green plaque records that this community (Oldbury) is recorded in the Domesday Book of 1086.

At the road go right and follow it until passing Manor Farm Lane just after which you will see a stile on the left side of the road. Cross the stile

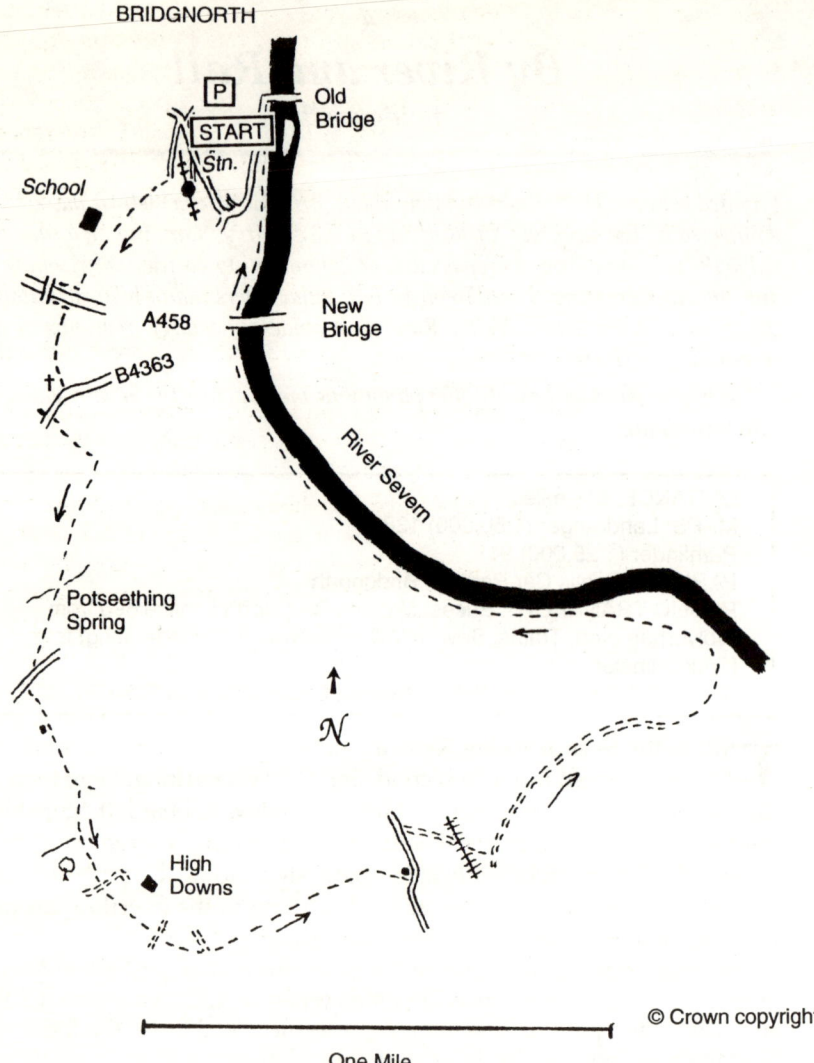

and walk down the field for 250 yards, with the hedge on your left, until arriving at a line of trees. To the left is a stile and a footpath sign. Turn right with the line of trees – keeping them on your right – to meet another stile that you cross into a larger field.

The paths are well trodden in this area and your route across the field is quite distinct, unless the field has just been ploughed of course! In this event aim slightly left towards a power pole and this bearing will bring you to another stile. Over this a few yards will bring you to yet another stile and a footbridge over the delightfully named Potseething Spring.

On the other side of the footbridge enter a field and walk diagonally across the centre aiming for the white gable end of a large house. As you arrive at the road near the house you will see a step stile in the fence. Go over and join the road. Turning right follow the road for 70 yards, passing the house, when you will see a step stile and public footpath sign on your left. Cross over into a small field and walk to the opposite left corner where there is a stile next to a gate.

This field sometimes contains a small flock of Jacob sheep, an ancient breed dating from biblical times.

In the next field follow the left hedge to another stile just in front of a white cottage. Over this now walk between the hedge and the cottage where the path soon becomes hedged and fenced. Arriving at another step stile cross it into another field and follow the same line, with the hedge on your left, to a double stile that leads into a large field.

Now cross this field (190 degrees) to the nearest, protruding corner of woodland ahead. On reaching the boundary fence do not cross it into the trees but instead bear left and follow the field edge, keeping the trees on your right, to the corner where a stile takes you onto a green lane. Cross the lane to the stile opposite and enter another field. Again the path is quite well trodden but should this not be the case then a bearing of 130 degrees will bring you to a stile at the side of a gate into the end of another green lane. Cross to the stile opposite and in the next field go very slightly left (110 degrees) to a stile in the fence ahead. Go over this and the one a few yards ahead to enter yet another lane, this time surfaced.

Opposite is a metal gate in the hedge that serves as a stile. On the other side go forward and through the gated hedge gap a few yards ahead. Now on a bearing of 65 degrees walk across the field, left of both a power pole and an oak tree, to arrive at a step stile in a short wooden section of fence.

Go over this stile but do not walk forward, instead go immediately right to another step stile in the same corner. This can sometimes be overgrown and may easily be missed. Now in the next field walk half left (60 degrees) to pass well right of an oak tree when you will see the protruding corner of a hedge and fence ahead. At the protruding corner continue forward along the narrower part of the field now with the hedge and fence on your right. Pass through a gate in the corner and then continue forward to a second gate and fence stile next to a power pole. Over this continue forward to a step stile well right of a metal gate. This takes you into an orchard where you now walk forward, and slightly right, to pass immediately right of the garden fence belonging to the white cottage. This brings you to a gate that you pass through to walk along the side of the cottage to a road.

Level Crossing on the Severn Valley Railway

On the road turn left and follow it a short distance until meeting a public footpath sign pointing right. This is just before another sign pointing to the Village Hall. Turn right, initially on tarmac and then on a green lane, to arrive at a SVR level crossing. Take care crossing the railway and on the other side continue forward on a distinct path to a T-junction with the fenced, unsurfaced Slade Lane. Here turn left and follow it on its approach to the River Severn.

In a while Slade Lane empties into a field and becomes a track that swings right – right of trees – along a shallow valley. Arriving at a gate at the side of the water treatment plant go through and turn immediately left along the top edge of the field with the fence on your left and below an embankment. Following the edge of this large field will eventually bring you to a stile at the riverside that you now cross.

Now you can put your map away and enjoy the next couple of riverside miles all the way back to the old river bridge at Bridgnorth.

Stoat

5
By Eckington!
Great Comberton

An attractive village on the River Avon with a tasteful mix of old thatch and new brick, Great Comberton is the start for this invigorating walk which has Bredon Hill as its focal point.
The village is probably unique in that it has neither a shop or a pub!

DISTANCE: 6½ miles
MAPS: Landranger (1:50,000) 150. Pathfinder (1:25,000) 1019 & 1042
PARKING: Roadside in Great Comberton plus a small 'lay-by' near Woollas Hall Farm (GR 945412)
START/FINISH: Lane at the rear of Great Comberton Church GR 955421

WITH your back to the rear of the church go left down the lane to turn right into Russell Street, a signed 'No through road'. Beyond an ancient, but sadly collapsing, barn; where part of the original wattle and daub can still be seen; the tarmac ends and becomes an unsurfaced lane. Continue forward along this bridleway which after a while consists of the left hedge only and then passes into a field where it follows the right hedge. A short distance after entering a second field your clear bridleway makes a sudden left turn to cross the field and meet the opposite hedge. Here the bridleway continues forward through the hedge – now as a hedged green lane – bringing you to a broad crossing track.

Turn right to follow the track gently upwards where in a short while it becomes fenced and then enters woodland right of a gate. Join and continue forward along a broad forestry road for the short distance to another gate. Do not go through the gate instead leave the forestry road by going left up a wide and, initially, fenced path. Follow this through the trees all the way to a hunter's gate which takes you onto the edge of an open plateau named Even Hill.

Here go straight across to the gate, hunter's gate and fence stile opposite. On the other side continue forward and up to meet the left hand fence surrounding trees. Follow the fence upwards to quickly veer away from it on a clear and delightfully grassy track which crosses rough pasture. In a while you will arrive at a gate on the edge of more woodland in front of which there is an obvious crossing track. Do not go through the gate, instead turn right along the crossing track and follow it along the fence for about 40 yards to its slightly protruding corner. Leave the fence to go forward and up for some 35 yards on a section of eroded track to meet a crossing grass track. To your left and upwards is the top corner of the woodland with a fence gate while to your right the broad grassy track rises gently above scrub bushes.

Go right on the grassy track and follow it to soon meet and follow a left fence with the escarpment to your right. This will take you right of a stand of pines to reach a gate. Through the gate continue forward with the right hand dry stone wall to meet the outer ditch and dyke of the hill fort. Stay with

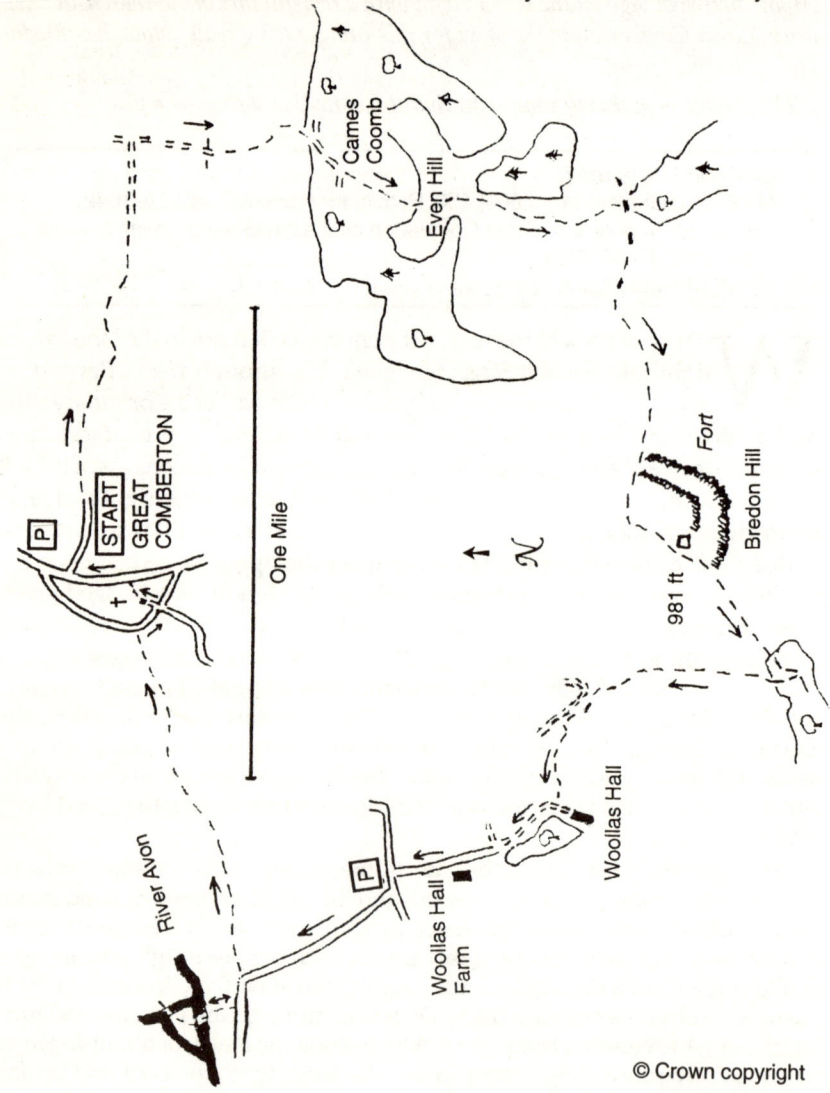

© Crown copyright

the wall to pass the inner ditch and dyke and so reach the Banbury Stone and tower.

Bredon Hill is an 'outlier' of the Cotswolds, the largest of several outcrops consisting of the same honey coloured oolitic limestone: the intervening land consists of softer materials and has been eroded away over the millennium. Standing at 981 feet – its tower was originally built to raise the height to a more dignified 1000 feet! – the hill offers a wide panorama to the Clee, Malvern and Cotswold Hills as well as across the Midland lowlands.

The hill fort is some 2000 years old and a good example of a natural feature – the escarpment – being utilised in a defensive position; the circle is completed by the well preserved double ditch and dyke. Human remains have been found here and are believed to be those of defenders against the Romans.

Surrounded by legend the origins of the Banbury Stone are geologic rather than mythical. Consisting of conglomerated limestone it evidences fracturing of the limestone – possibly scree – cemented together by calcitic water.

On a more mundane level, Bredon Hill is the half way stage of this walk and as such provides an excellent spot for rest and refreshment – though you should have brought your own!

Leaving the fort continue following the wall to pass the other end of the outer ditch and dyke. Here go through a gate to continue with the wall to the field corner and its junction with another wall in front of trees. Near the corner there is a gate which takes you into the woodland where you follow a track through the trees. In about 100 yards, immediately after a left bend and adjacent to a gate on the left, a path goes off right down to a metal gate in a wall. Go down to it where you will see the gate has a metal step. Cross over to follow the clear path down to a crossing track where there are two upright stone pillars, formerly used as gate posts.

Immediately left of these stones is a field gate. Pass through it into a sloping pasture and initially go left with a line of stunted trees and a broken wall, keeping them on your left. In some 50 yards swing right to follow the grassy line of a vehicle track which is initially a line heading for the bottom left corner of a conifer plantation in the distance. Just before reaching a tree lined water course your track swings left and down to then swing right to the bottom right corner of the pasture. Here a gated step stile takes you over the culverted stream and past a water trough to a bend in a farm road. Go left along the unsurfaced road to a gate.

Through the gate go left to regain the near bank of the stream and follow it down. Soon you will see a step stile which takes you onto the tarmac drive in front of a cattle grid and the entrance to Woollas Hall. Leaving the large and impressive hall behind go right on the tarmac and follow it all the way down, passing right of Woollas Hall Farm, to join a road at a T-junction. Turn left and then quickly right along the road signed for Nafford and Eckington.

After almost half a mile the road makes a very sharp left bend. On the right of the bend is a gated step stile and a public footpath sign which indicates your way back to Great Comberton.

At this point it is interesting to make a short diversion to Nafford lock and weirs where footbridges carry a public footpath across the River Avon. To achieve this simply follow the left bend and in about 100 yards go right down the signed footpath to the river. The area of the lock and weirs has plenty of interest but do keep a close rein on children. Having had a look around return to the south bank and retrace your steps to the sharp bend noted earlier – see sketch map.

On the bend cross the step stile and follow the direction of the footpath sign straight ahead for a long field crossing.

Though usually under crops the path is often used, well trodden and should present no difficulties unless you are unfortunate enough to walk it immediately after ploughing. In this circumstance a bearing of 85 degrees – and initially some 50 yards parallel to the left boundary – will bring you to your next objective which is a footbridge in the opposite boundary.

Arriving at the footbridge cross it into another field and follow the left hedge/fence. About 40 yards before the next corner go left down a low embankment to a step stile. Cross it and resume your original line, now with the fence on your right to its protruding corner at an oak tree. Here go forward to a second oak and then swing right along a just discernible track which descends to a gated step stile and sleeper bridge. On the other side rise along the wide break between wire fencing left and wooden ranch fencing right. This will bring you to another gated step stile between houses and so onto the road in Great Comberton.

Turn right along the road and then left at the junction opposite the village hall where you go immediately left again, next to the road signs, along an enclosed footpath which takes you into the churchyard.

A look at the churchyard's magnificent and ancient yew – with some of its branches propped for support – is an appropriate end to a historic walk.

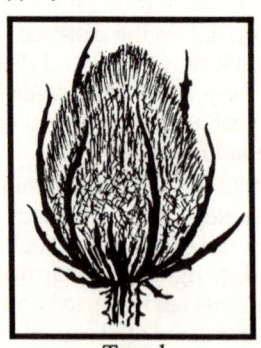

Teasel

6
The Suckley Hills
Lulsley

Approximately eight miles west of Worcester there is a chain of hills that run north to south from the Wyre Forest to the Malverns. Such is the nature of these hills that it can be argued that they form the natural northern outliers to the Malverns. The Suckley Hills, which this walk explores, certainly form a superbly wooded ridge walk and provide outstanding views across this rural part of Worcestershire. Orchards, Oast Houses and patchwork patterned field systems are all well viewed from these higher level footpaths.

The walk starts from the Ravenshill Wood Nature Reserve which is in the care of the Worcestershire Nature Conservation Trust and which supports a wide range of bird and plant life – not least being Herb Paris, one of Worcestershire's rare plants.

DISTANCE: 7 miles
MAPS: Landranger (1:50,000) 149 & 150. Pathfinder (1:25,000) 995
PARKING: Ravenshill Wood Nature Reserve and Picnic Site (GR 740540)
PUBLIC TRANSPORT: Midland Red West Express Service or British Rail to Worcester. Midland Red West from Worcester (services 421 & 422 – except Saturday & Sunday) to Longley Green. Join walk from Longley Green.
START/FINISH: Ravenshill Wood Nature Reserve and Picnic Site (GR 740540)

LEAVE the Nature Reserve and return to the road where you now turn left. In just over 100 yards you will come to a road junction, the boundary sign for Lulsley and, on the left, a public footpath sign. Turn left to follow the direction of the sign along the hedged footpath and so reach a step stile into woodland. Entering the trees follow a clear path until it brings you to a T-junction with a broad track. Go left with the track until reaching another junction of tracks where you go left again to reach another step stile. Over the stile a path will bring you to the left of a house. Walk left along the drive from the house where in just a few yards you will see a sign 'bridleway' directing you right and down. Follow the sign down to shortly reach a junction with a crossing path. Here go left to follow the enclosed path to houses.

Ridges and Valleys III

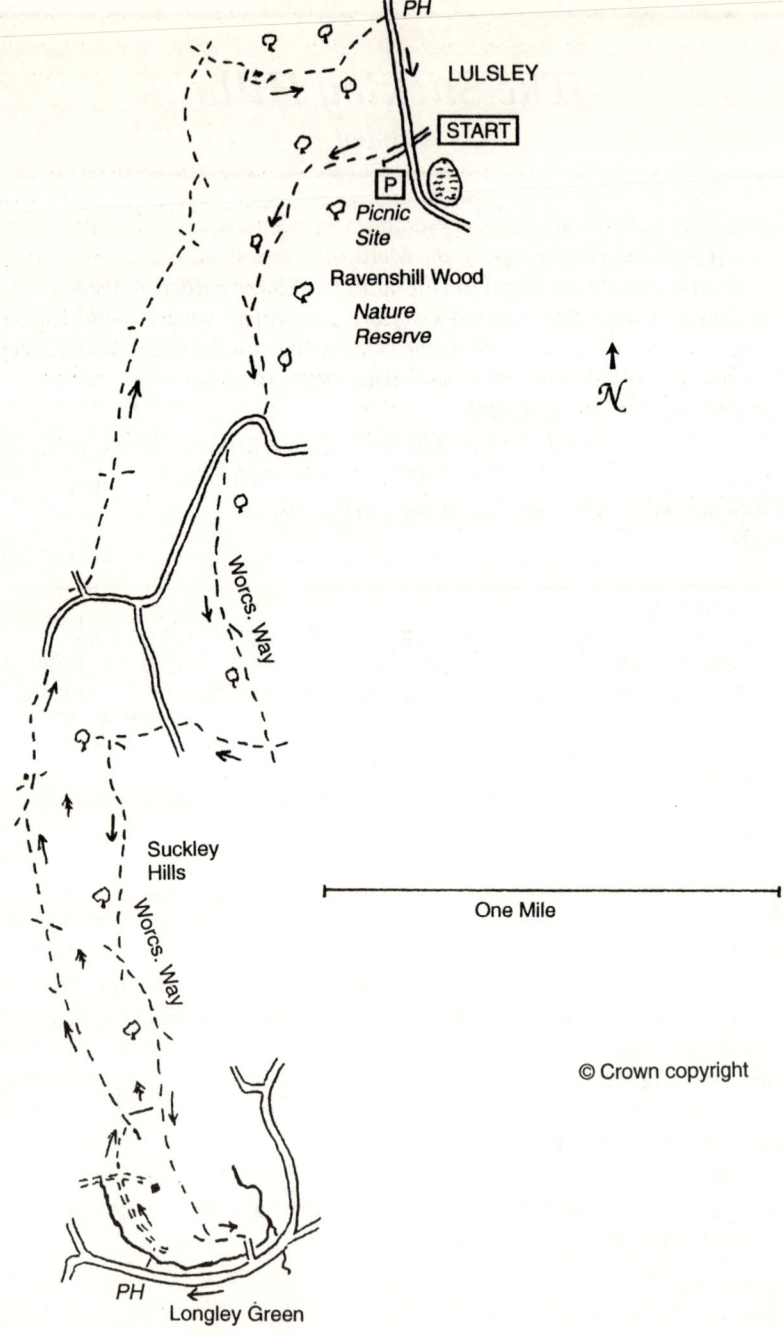

You are now on the Worcestershire Way (WW) a long distance regional path created by the County Council and which runs from Kinver Edge to the Malvern Hills – a distance of some thirty-six miles. Your walk now takes advantage of the WW as far as Longley Green and, not surprisingly, up to that point your route is well waymarked.

At the houses walk forward and down along an unsurfaced service road that brings you to a metalled lane. At the lane go right and follow it around a left bend where on the left you will meet a footpath sign and waymark posts. Turn left with the sign and follow the woodland track until you come to a junction of paths. At the junction a marker post and yellow arrow point you right, while a few yards ahead a sign high on a tree declares: 'Warning. Dogs worrying livestock will be shot. Keep to paths. Keep your dog on a lead'. Here turn right with the yellow arrow and follow the broad ridge top path to a gated stile. Continue forward and quickly arrive at a small clearing where a track goes left and down while you continue forward and up with the WW arrow. After some distance and immediately after cresting the highest point you will come to another waymarker post and another small clearing.

Ahead, through the avenue of trees, are outstanding views of the Malvern Hills.

At the clearing go right with the WW arrow to quickly pass two signed requests 'Please keep dogs on Leads' and 'Please keep to Footpaths'. Follow the track as it descends to a gated stile and a surfaced lane. Cross the lane to the gated stile on the other side and so enter an orchard where you now walk forward with a hedge to your right and the fruit trees to your left. Quickly arriving at another waymarked and gated stile into woodland walk forward to meet a forestry track. At the junction go right for just a few yards and then leave the forestry road by swinging left with the WW marker along and up a broad, well walked path.

The path quickly swings south and now follows the beautifully wooded ridge of the Suckley Hills which again offer good views of the Malverns and the attractive surrounding countryside. After a while you will come to a broad crossing bridle track. Here go left and down to arrive at a gate on the woodland edge. The scene to the valley bottom ahead is quite magnetic but do not go through the gate, instead turn right with the WW arrow to follow the woodland edge. In a while pass through a hunter's gate and continue on the clear path until reaching a junction of paths. Here keep left and down and in a few yards arrive at a gate. To the left of the gate is a fence stile that you cross to go immediately right and down to a metal hunter's gate in the bottom corner next to a sign 'Beware. Fast Horses'.

Go through the gate and turn right to cross the fenced gallop and so pass through the gap on the other side to a white metal gate. Through the gate, and towards the rear of a house, cross the stream bridge and follow the enclosed path at the side of the house to reach the road at Longley Green.

Turn right along the road and follow it as far as The Nelson public house. On the right, opposite the pub sign, there is a step stile into a field. Cross into the field and follow the right hand edge down to the stream where a plank footbridge followed by a railed footbridge take you to the other side. Here you join the continuation of the fenced gallop that you crossed earlier.

Go left with the gallop, soon leaving the trees, to enter a pasture where the gallop is fenced on both sides.

Here the OS and definitive maps show the path going through the corner of the right hand wooden fence and following a line diagonally up the slope to follow a garden wall to a gate onto the drive in front of the house – 'Grove Hill'. From here the right of way goes left and down the drive where, in a few yards and immediately before the bridge, it meets the gate to the gallop (left). However, at the time of writing, the path line was effectively obstructed by the aforementioned fence which was topped with barbed wire. As the right of way runs almost parallel to, and just a few yards away from, the fenced gallop this very short section is now described as the practical expedient.

Continue with the fenced gallop (Beware of Fast Horses again!)and follow it to meet the crossing drive that leads to the house up on the right. Cross the drive and go through the gate opposite to then quickly pass through a second gate. Immediately through this second gate and before a barn cross the ranch fencing on the right and go half left across the sloping pasture to meet the line of a bridleway where you go left for the few yards to a hunter's gate at the bottom corner of woodland. Go through the hunter's gate and follow the top field edge, with the woodland on your right, to the point where the woodland fence swings right.

At this protruding corner continue forward, veering slightly left, to pass well left of a solitary tree and so meet the bottom fence just before a crossing fence. In this bottom left fence you will see a metal gate that you pass through to enter a field. At the field edge take the upper right boundary and follow the fence and hedge, keeping it on your right. Passing a gate you will come to the protruding corner of the hedge where you leave it to go directly forward across the field aiming for the gate ahead, left of a house.

Passing through the gate join a track to go right towards the house. Immediately before the gate in front of the house cross the step stile on the right and follow the garden boundary fence to its corner. Here go left and pass right of the house, still following the garden fence, to the next corner. At this corner strike forward and slightly right across the slope of the large field to a protruding corner in the opposite hedge/fence where there is a large holly bush. Here walk the few yards forward to the inverted corner where there is a gate and a bridleway sign. Go through the gate and follow the hedged track, past buildings, to enter a hedged green lane. Now follow the green lane to a T-junction with a surfaced lane near cottages.

The path through Green Hill woods

At the surfaced lane go left for about fifteen yards where you will see public footpath signs and gates both left and right. Taking the one on the right – and quickly crossing a track – walk forward and up the slope of a ridge to a hunter's gate left of a gas pipeline marker post. Pass through the hunter's gate and walk between the new plantings left and a fence right as the lovely grassy track develops into a stunning ridge walk.

The evidence of stone paving protruding through the turf would suggest that this is probably an ancient trackway.

Further along the ridge, and nearer the top, your track forks. You take the right, higher one thus staying with the right hand fence. Soon you will arrive at a gate that takes your track through woodland and then out at the other side via a hunter's gate. Continue forward with the right hand fence – passing two Scots pines left – to a gate in the top field corner. In the next field follow the same line, still with the right hand fence, to reach the top of a mound. *In the distance can be seen the Clee Hills.* At the top of the mound go over the gated step stile in the fence corner and follow the fence surrounding new plantings to its protruding corner. Here strike half right down the field to the bottom far right corner where a wooden hunter's gate awaits you.

Go through the hunter's gate and shortly through another into pasture. In the pasture go half right to follow the top of the field with a low embankment of trees on your right. Staying with the top of the field and the embankment of trees follow it as it swings right – near a stunted tree with a clump of mistletoe – up to a fence gap and onto a track between two gates. Here go through the left hand gate – you are now back on the Worcestershire Way – and follow a fine grassy track still with the trees and embankment on your right. Staying with the right hand line of trees will bring you towards a line of conifer trees and under power lines next to double wooden poles. Immediately in front and right there are double wooden gates carrying blue WW bridleway signs. Pass through them and follow the left hand hedge to the next top corner where there is a hunter's gate adjacent to another set of double wooden power poles.

Do not go through the hunter's gate, instead go right under the power lines – with the hedge on your left – to the gate in the next corner. Pass through the gate and quickly through a second to pass between two barns where you immediately turn right to a gate with a footpath sign next to it. Go through into an orchard to pass right of the house and its garden and so arrive at another gate leading onto the house drive. Through the gate go forward along the drive – which soon becomes surfaced – as it takes you down through woodland.

In Spring this drive is lined with a profusion of daffodils and tulips.

Now simply follow the drive all the way down to the road at Lulsley where to the left is the Fox and Hounds pub. To return to the car park and picnic area simply go right along the road and so back to the Nature Reserve.

7

Riding the Range
Cannock Chase

There are at least three separate 'Seven Springs' on Cannock Chase: this walk starts from the northernmost. Rising through Abraham's Valley to a height of 654 feet, and then following part of the Sherbrook Valley, it is an outstanding mix of forest and heathland. Mostly on Forestry Commission land the walk exclusively follows public bridleways: consequently, should the threat of privatisation eventually overtake the Commission, this walk will remain perfectly valid.

By using one or other of the optional parking places the walk can be split into two shorter circuits for those who have less time available – the triangulation pillar being the fulcrum.

DISTANCE: 7½ miles
MAPS: Landranger (1:50,000) 127 & 128. Pathfinder (1:25,000) 850, 851, 871 & 872.
PARKING: Just off the A513 at Seven Springs Car Park and Picnic Area (GR 004206) or the car park near the entrance to the ACF buildings and Rifle Ranges (GR 999173).
PUBLIC TRANSPORT: Midland Red West services X25, 823, 825 (Tamworth-Lichfield-Stafford). Alight for Seven Springs.
START/FINISH: The walk is described using Seven Springs Car Park and Picnic Area as the start and finish, though the walk can just as easily be started from the car park near Rifle Range Corner.

AT SEVEN SPRINGS, with your back to the A513, go through the left hand of the two vehicle barriers in front and follow the broad track across the grassy picnic area. Quickly entering trees the track swings right in front of a fence – on the other side are pools – and then follows it in a generally southward direction.

In a while you will reach another vehicle barrier, where another track comes in from the right. Here continue forward along the valley with a stream down on your left. Shortly arriving at another junction, ignore the left branch and continue forward. Here the stream has left you for a short while but soon returns to accompany you as you gradually ascend Abraham's Valley. Ignoring side tracks stay with the main one for another mile until arriving at a T-junction with a crossing forestry road. In front is a flag pole and a Rifle Range warning sign. Here, to avoid the range, go right along the forestry road and soon arrive at a cross roads. Cross over and

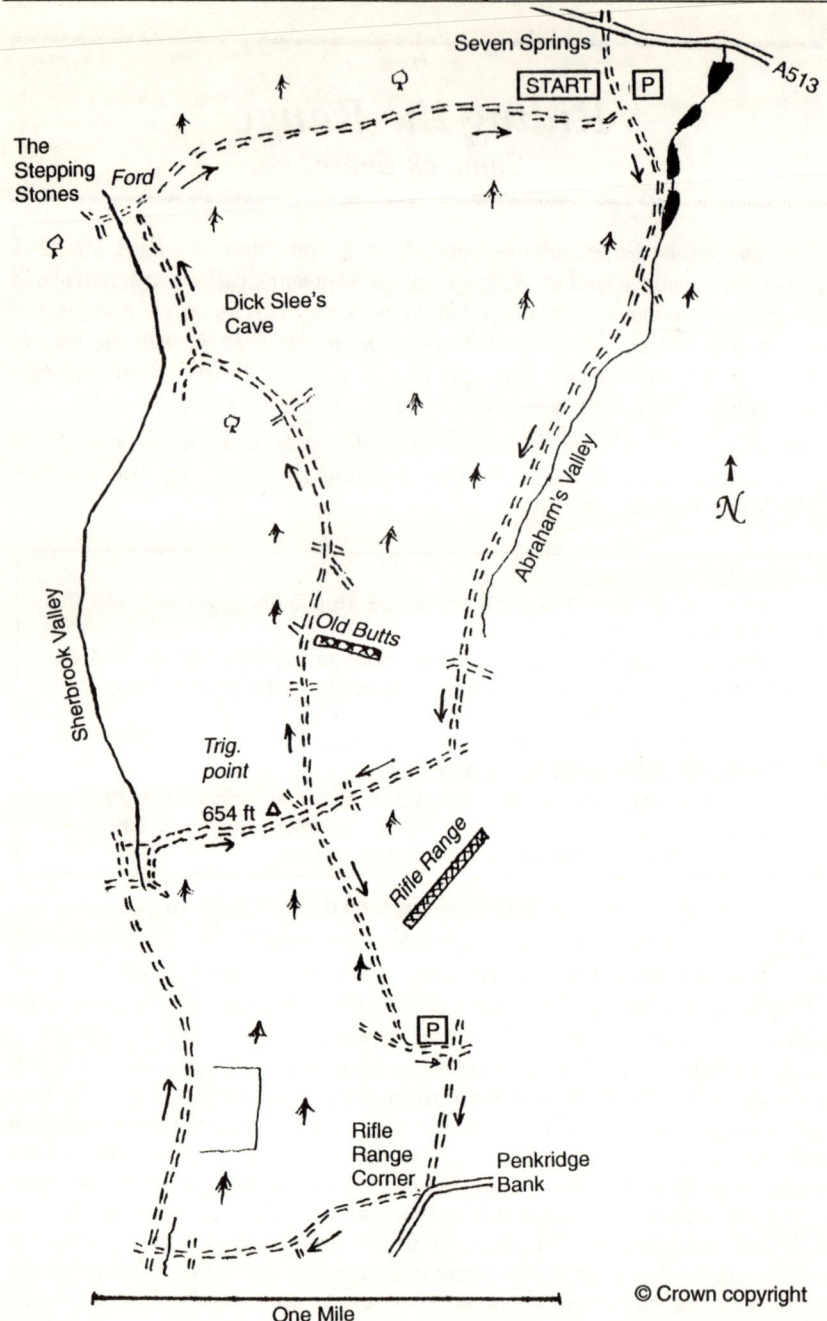

continue forward to quickly come to another junction of tracks just before the triangulation pillar.

Turn left and follow the straight, broad track to reach another vehicle barrier. Go through this – there are brick buildings to the left – and arrive at another T-junction with a crossing track. Here go left and pass a parking area near the gate to the ACF buildings. Immediately past this you will come to a crossing, broad, unsurfaced road that comes from the Rifle Range. Go right and follow it all the way to a tarmac road on a bend – Rifle Range Corner.

Immediately before the tarmac road go right, through a vehicle barrier, and follow the forestry road. Again, ignoring side tracks, follow it all the way into the bottom of the Sherbrook Valley. Here go over the crossing track on the nearside of the stream and go forward the few yards over the stream to the wooden marker post on the opposite bank. Here turn right and follow the watercourse down stream (signed for 'The Stepping Stones 2m') for about three quarters of a mile when you will come to a crossing track which fords the stream and where there are stepping stones – *not the Stepping Stones of the sign post.*

At the crossing track continue forward on the left hand side of the stream for another 100 yards. Here, when you are adjacent to the corner of the woodland across the stream, you will see a path that descends to a sleeper footbridge. Turn right to follow it across the stream and then rise to join a track on a bend at the corner of the trees.

Go forward and up the track with the trees on your right and heathland on your left. After a fairly steep climb you will arrive back at the triangulation pillar and the cross-road of tracks. Here there are two tracks going left. One follows the edge of the woodland and the other enters the trees. Take the second of these left tracks and follow it through the trees to soon cross a crossing track and then arrive at the old butts – a man-made sand and gravel bank. Passing immediately left of the butts ignore the left branch in the track and go forward, bearing slightly right. Now gradually descending and ignoring side tracks follow this direction all the way back into the Sherbrook Valley. Here your track swings right to follow the line of the stream all the way to the picnic area, near the ford and the Stepping Stones, where you T-junction with a crossing track.

Just before reaching the picnic area – up to the right and out of sight – is Dick Slee's Cave, the site of a hermit's hut.

At the T-junction go right along the track with a woodland fence on the left. Again ignoring side tracks; follow this track for just over a mile, all the way back to the Seven Springs car park.

8
A Walk that has the Edge
Brown Edge

As the focal point of Greenway Bank Country Park, Knypersley Reservoir is an impressive 'two tier' expanse of water supplying both the Caldon and the Trent and Mersey canals. It is a fitting start and conclusion for this most varied circular walk that in part follows the infant River Trent, the attractive Caldon Canal and the dramatic Staffordshire Moorland's Brown Edge.

> DISTANCE: 7¾ miles
> MAPS: Landranger (1:50,000) 118. Pathfinder (1:25,000) 792
> PARKING: Car Park and Picnic Area on the shore of Knypersley Reservoir. There is also a car parking area just below Marshes Hill, Brown Edge (GR 907546)
> PUBLIC TRANSPORT: PMT service 69 from Hanley to Brown Edge. If starting from Brown Edge make your way to the church and read from ➤ on page 34
> START/FINISH: Car Park and Picnic Area, Knypersley Reservoir (GR 894550)

LEAVING the car park go left to cross the dam where, just before the end and on the right, you will see a public footpath sign for Norton Green. Turning right descend steps and cross a footbridge between pools to then pass right of a weir. Now following the right bank of the stream cross a strange elongated step stile into another field where you continue with the stream – in fact the young River Trent – until reaching another footbridge. Cross over and walk forward, initially away from the Trent, to follow the left bank of what appears to be an overflow channel.

In reality the overflow channel is a canal feeder which you now follow 'on and off', virtually all the way to the Caldon Canal.

Passing through a wooden squeeze stile, and then two more, now follow a raised bank between the Trent on the right and the feeder left. *Up to the left can be seen the radio mast on the top of Brown Edge which, later in the day, you will pass.* This path will soon bring you to a surfaced lane that you cross to continue the same direction along the slightly raised bank of the feeder. In a little while the feeder goes underground – with any overflow going right into the river. Here continue forward, through a stile, and in about 75 yards meet the feeder again as it emerges from its culvert. Staying with the right bank follow it to a point where it swings sharply left. Here

A Walk that has the Edge

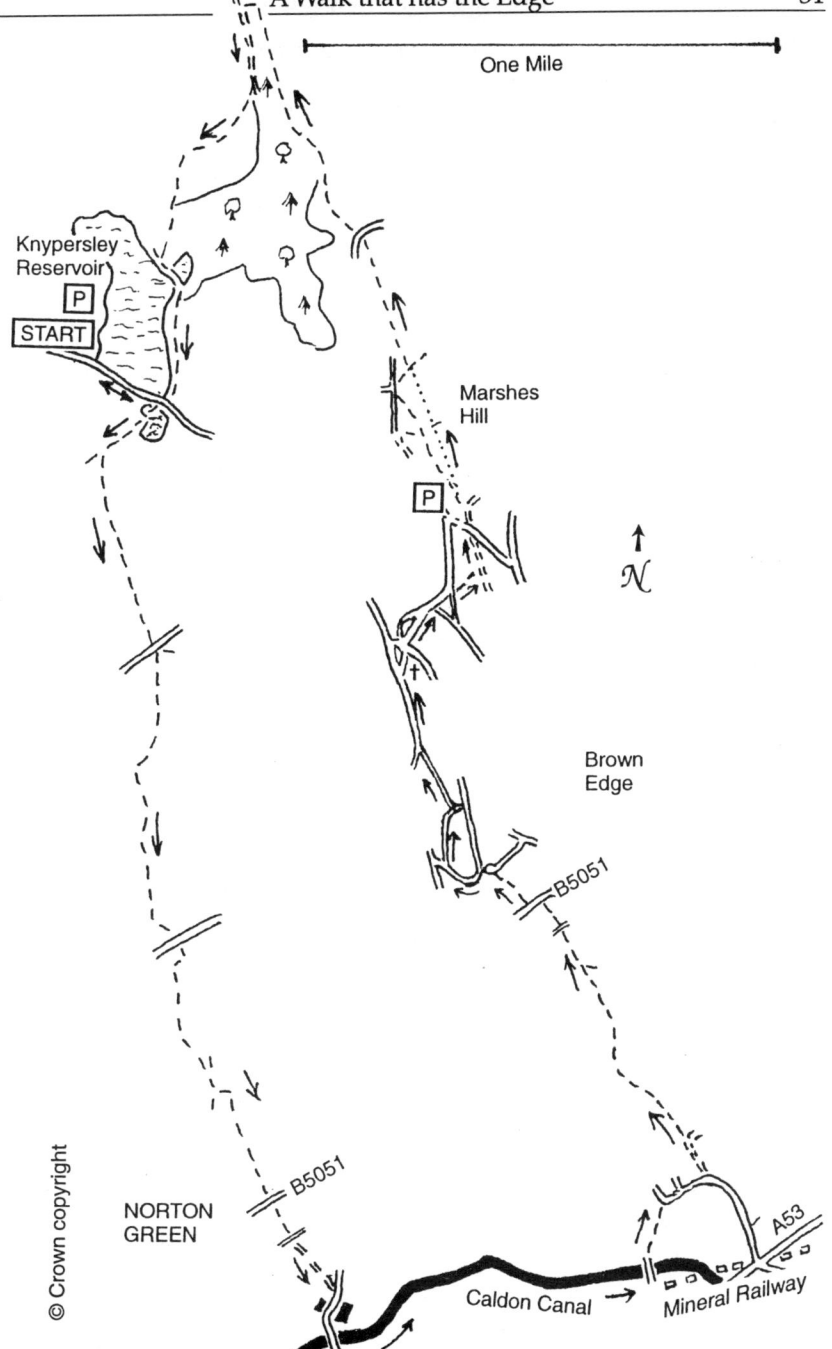

31

One Mile

Knypersley Reservoir
P
START

Marshes Hill

P

N

Brown Edge

B5051

© Crown copyright

NORTON GREEN

B5051

Caldon Canal

A53

Mineral Railway

cross a tractor bridge and follow the opposite bank for 60 yards to meet a tarmac lane at a footpath sign.

Turn right along the lane and in 35 yards go left with the public footpath sign, up steps, to meet your old friend the re-emergent feeder which promptly disappears again. Here walk forward to the wooden stile in the corner of a barbed wire fence. Over this follow the field edge with the fence on your right and in the next corner cross another stile where you now go straight ahead to meet a stone pillared gateway and the feeder again. Go through the stone squeeze stile in the gateway and forward with the feeder on your left. Soon the feeder disappears again and you continue ahead to pick up and follow a left hand fence. Arriving at a protruding corner go left and then right along the field edge to a wooden step stile. Cross the step stile and walk forward with the hedge and the feeder on your left to the end of the field where at the corner you meet larch-lap fencing. In the corner cross the step stile left and then the one immediately right next to a lamp post.

Lift bridge on the Caldon Canal

At the lamp post go straight ahead along the concrete footpath to meet a road at a Newsagents and Off Licence. Cross the road to follow the left edge of an open space next to the garden hedges. Soon cross another road to follow the farm road opposite which brings you to a gate in front of Heakley Hall Farm. Go through the gate and at the end of a 'prefab' swing right, to pass right of the farm buildings, and then follow a stone wall to a field gate next to a large tree. Pass through the gate and follow the left wall and hedge to cross the bridge over the Caldon Canal. Go right down the steps onto the towpath and right again under the bridge to now follow the canal in a easterly direction.

Opened in 1779 the Caldon Canal was designed to transport the vast quantities of limestone extracted from the Caldon Low quarries near Froghall. Tramways were constructed from the quarries to Froghall Basin where the limestone was transhipped into barges for transportation onto the countrywide canal network. Though not visited on this walk, there is a picnic area at Froghall Wharf where the industrial archeologist can have a wonderful time – it is worth a visit.

As you walk the towpath you will pass a drawbridge and then a lock (number 5) where on the opposite bank there is a pumping station. A short distance after lock 5 you will come to a brick bridge immediately before lock 6. Here you leave the canal to cross the bridge and where the track swings left to the pumping station you leave it on the bend to go straight ahead to the wooden squeeze stile just right of a gate. Through the stile follow the clear path and the right hand fence up to meet a wooden wicket gate. Through this, and still with the right hand fence, follow the edge of a large lawn to meet the public footpath sign at a bend in a surfaced lane.

Go right with the lane (Edgefield Lane) to pass Willfield Lane and so quickly meet another lane junction at a right bend. Here go left with the footpath sign up the surfaced lane to where it swings right at 'Greenroofs'. Leave the tarmac on the bend to go forward to the gated squeeze stile and so enter a field.

Now begins a steady climb for just over a third of a mile. Along this section you will notice trees up to the right. This is in fact Tinster Wood and though it is higher and has a right of way running parallel to yours, it is not really worth visiting for the potential views are completely obliterated by tree cover. Your route at least offers views to the left, and there is better to come!

In this sloping field walk forward and up with the remains of a left hand stone wall that soon gives way to a fence. Crossing a stile you continue up with the left fence, now accompanied by the wall again. Cresting the rise near a large holly bush you will see the 'terraced' village of Brown Edge spread before you. Continue forward to reach a gated step stile and over it follow the farm track forward to cross a cattle grid and pass between houses to a road. Cross the road to the metal step stile and gate opposite where you follow a wide path and the left stone wall to reach the B5051 in front of a shop.

Turn left along the B5051 and immediately before the Hollybush pub go right with the signed footpath across playing fields. This will bring you between houses to the end of a cul-de-sac. Here you cross over to go left along the enclosed path between numbers 9a and 10 to reach another road.

Here you are near the older parts of Brown Edge. This multi-level upland village was once a mining community that is now a blend of old industrial village and modern architecture. The way it is built, on the slopes of Brown Edge, make it a fascinating place with lots of 'hidden' byways, some of which you will now follow. The parish church of St. Anne – the patron saint of miners – celebrated its 150th anniversary in 1994.

Meeting the road, in front of 'The Bungalow' and 'Three Gables', go left and follow it as it soon swings right below a grassy embankment to meet another road at a T-junction. Immediately before the T-junction and on the right is a stone cottage (No. 18 Hillview) that carries a sign 'Bank End'. Next to it is a narrow lane named Back Lane. Turn right into Back Lane and follow it as it rises and then narrows to climb steps at the side of a bungalow – 'Les Fleurs' – after which you descend towards a road. Do not join the road but instead turn acutely left along the narrow tarmac signed 'The Rocks'. Follow this up as it rises and passes immediately right of number 6 to become a narrow stone walled lane that contours with nice views left.

Soon descending to a junction with a road, opposite Lingfield Avenue, turn right and follow it (Church Road) to pass immediately left of St. Anne's church.

➤ *Start from here if using public transport.*

Here stay with the road as it swings right – signed Knypersley 3¼ – and becomes New Lane. Follow it past a school and rise towards the radio mast. Almost at the top of New Lane – just before the radio mast and the sign for Top Chapel Lane – go right at a footpath sign next to a wall corner and up steps onto Top Chapel Lane. Here take the second (upper) right turn for just a few yards to a gate behind a house. Before the gate turn left through a gap in the wall and follow the gravel path up to pass left of the radio mast and so enter another narrow surfaced lane at a public footpath sign.

Go left with this lane to a crossing road and then straight across to follow another public footpath sign. Follow the unfenced tarmac to the car parking area on the left just before a gate marked 'Private'. Go half left across the parking area to a kissing gate and onto the heathland of Marshes Hill. Walk up to the summit where there is a bench seat and the remains of a rectangular pillar.

On the summit (899 feet) you have fine views in all directions across the Staffordshire Moorlands. To the north-east and on the skyline can be seen – in good visibility – the sham castle on Mow Cop. This forms the county boundary between Cheshire and Staffordshire and is of particular interest as the start of two long distance footpaths – the Staffordshire Way (92 miles) and the Gritstone Trail (18½ miles).

While the map shows the right of way following the left flank of Marshes Hill, just below the summit, there is a well trodden permissive route along the top which is now described – see the dotted line on the sketch map.

From the bench seat and pillar follow the path north along the highest part of the ridge. Just before the end of the heathland go over a crossing path and forward with a right hand stone wall. Soon your path merges with a track near a wind pump and then passes right of a cottage. Just beyond the cottage your way forward is now a green path between stone walls. This takes you through a stone squeeze stile and forward with a left hand stone wall to its protruding corner. Here continue forward along the top as your grassy way descends towards buildings at the foot of the hill. This will bring you to a gated squeeze stile onto a surfaced lane.

Cross the lane to follow the farm drive in front. Passing between a house right and a garage left, bear left down a grassy area – below a concrete road – to pass through a narrow gap between a barn (right) and a wooden fence (left). This will bring you into a field where you go forward and then gently down on a fairly clear path that descends to follow the infant Trent upstream along the valley bottom.

This is the Trent just a mile from its source and before it enters Knypersley Reservoir.

Soon arriving at a footbridge cross it and walk up the clear path with a tributary stream on your right. This soon brings you up to meet a stone wall on the left which you follow to a corner where there is a stepped squeeze stile next to a fenced gateway. Cross through to go right along the edge of the woodland keeping the stone wall on your right. Ahead you will see a bungalow and when adjacent to it your path starts to go left to T-junction with a crossing unsurfaced road.

Here go left along the unsurfaced road and follow it along the other edge of the woodland, in the opposite direction to that in which you have just travelled. Soon you will come to a dramatic rock outcrop and a pool. About 65 yards beyond the pool the unsurfaced road will bring you to a gate in the wall on the right. On the right edge of the gate is a wooden squeeze stile which you take to go half left, with the left hand fence, in a general south-westerly direction.

Soon, ahead and below, you will see Knypersley Reservoir shimmering in the sun light – we hope!

Arriving at a corner cross the stile and in the next field go directly across and down to a gateway next to a tree. On the right edge of this gateway is a stile that takes you onto the right side of a barbed wire fence. Keeping this fence on your left follow it in a southerly direction all the way down to the shore of the reservoir. Here go left along the lakeside track and follow it all the way to the road where you then go right across the dam and back to the car park. *If you are using public transport continue from page 30.*

*The historic Whittington Inn
(Walk 9)*

Common frog

9
Border Town
Kinver

This is how Kinver has been described and certainly one can imagine its strategic importance in days gone by. Dominated by cliffs and edges the area would plainly have been defensible from the earliest of times. A hill fort on the edge itself, together with the parish church high on a sandstone buttress, amply demonstrate this feature.

Once part of a royal hunting manor, and later an important staging post on a coaching route, Kinver is a fascinating place for exploration with many examples of old timbered buildings.

This walk explores Kinver's unique backwaters and, later, an equally fascinating spot high above the River Stour and the Staffordshire and Worcestershire Canal. You won't be sorry you came!

> DISTANCE: 8½ miles
> MAPS: Landranger (1:50,000) 138 & 139. Pathfinder (1:25,000) 933
> PARKING: Public car parks in Kinver
> PUBLIC TRANSPORT: Midland Red West service 242 from Stourbridge.
> START/FINISH: High Street, Kinver. Near the Public Library (GR 845834)

IN KINVER HIGH STREET locate the public library and follow the public footpath sign that points up towards it. Walk up the narrow surfaced road that passes in front of the library and in a short distance reach a parting of the ways. Of the three ways, the one straight ahead to the new church hall is waymarked as a public footpath. Though not waymarked the right-hand unsurfaced track, which carries a Private Drive sign, is also a public footpath – this is yours. So, going right follow this track up to a point where; on a bend, at a gate, and at the end of wooden fencing; you will see a public footpath sign on the left that takes you through a metal wicket gate and into a fenced and hedged path. Now follow this path until descending to meet a tarmac lane.

At the lane turn right and follow it past the entrance to the scout camp when in a short while you will come to a Y-junction with 'The Compa'. Here turn left and walk up the tarmac lane to pass 'Comber House' and then 'Morningside'. Just beyond 'Morningside' there is a lay-by with a vehicle barrier fence. Turn right through the fence and descend a path onto the open heathland of Kinver Edge (National Trust). At the bottom of the dip go over

Ridges and Valleys III

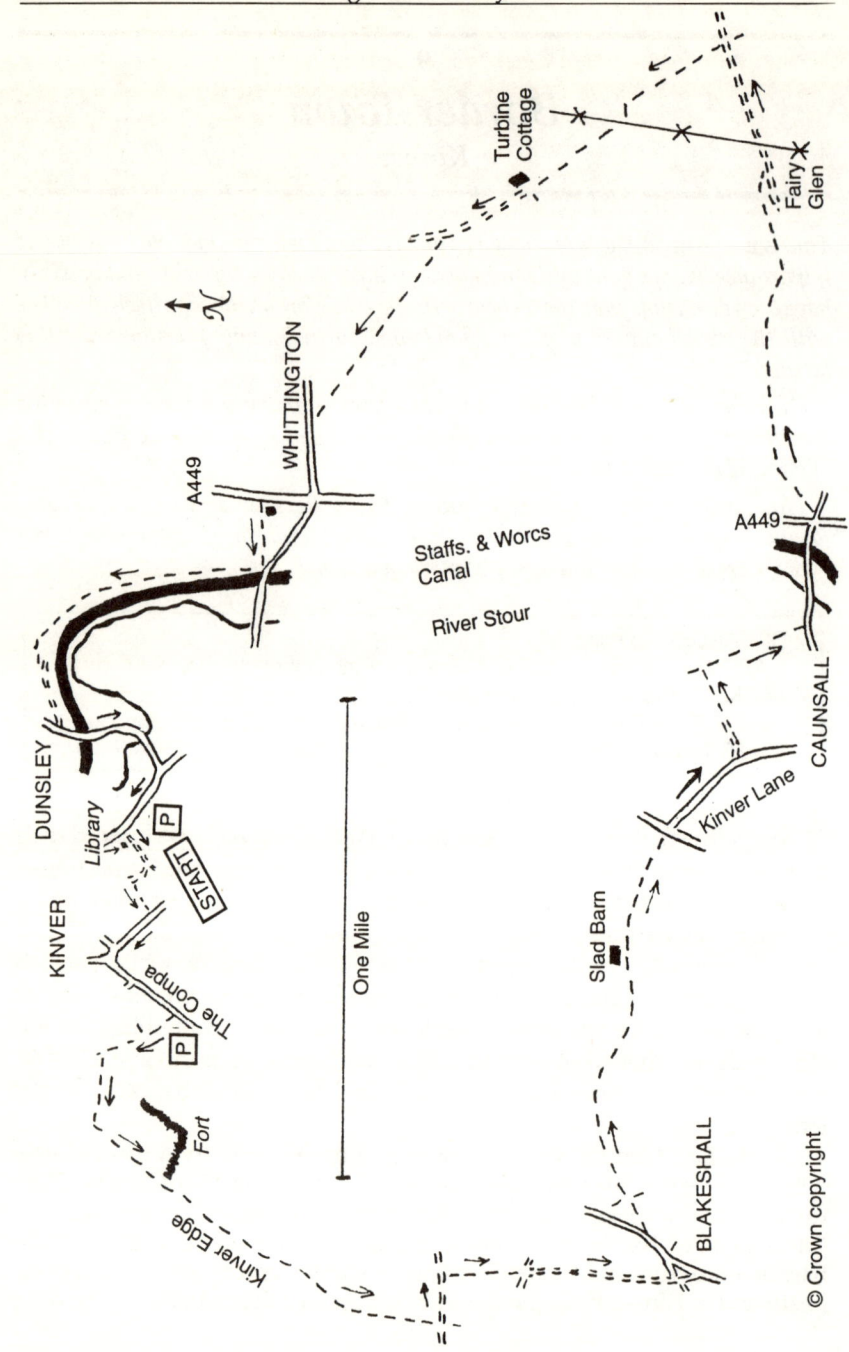

a crossing path and so up the main stepped path that takes you up to a grassy brow. *As a reference point, to the right and through the trees, you can just see a small conservatory.* To your left is a rising stepped path. Go left up the path and follow it to the toposcope on Kinver Edge itself. Here you can rest to take in the views identified on this visual aid.

Restored, now simply follow the edge and soon the Staffordshire Way markers. *Note the embankments of the hill fort to the left.* Further on you will come to the triangulation pillar marking the highest point of Kinver Edge, 538 feet. From here continue along the edge for some distance until coming to the signpost and display board showing the junction of three long distance footpaths; the Staffordshire Way (92 miles), the North Worcestershire Path (21 miles) and the Worcestershire Way (36 miles).

Here go left with the sign for the North Worcestershire Path (NWP) and follow the broad track down to wooden vehicle barriers where a NWP waymark post directs you right. Go right and shortly come to another NWP waymark post which directs you left: do NOT follow it on this occasion however, instead continue forward along the broad track, crossing other tracks and vehicle barriers on the way, until merging with a track coming in from the left. Continue forward to go through another vehicle barrier with a 'Horses' sign and so enter a hedged green lane. Follow the green lane to its end at a junction with a tarmac lane.

At this lane go left and in 75 yards pass a public bridleway sign on the right. Continue with the lane to soon arrive at another bridleway sign, again on the right. Go right to follow this broad way and soon arrive at a junction of tracks where your route goes straight ahead with the NWP waymark, along a fenced and then hedged bridleway which follows a line of power poles. After a while you will pass the outbuildings, and then the house itself, of Sladd Barn – so named on the map, though anything but a barn! Continuing with the hedged bridleway you will eventually come to a tarmac road opposite Kinver Lane.

Here leave the NWP by following Kinver Lane until arriving at an unsurfaced track on the left, just before houses and 30 mph signs. Go left with the track and follow it up to pass the edge of the houses and, on the right, an unmade road. Quickly reaching a gate into a field cross the stile at the side and then follow the same line with the fence on your right. In the next corner cross another step stile and in this next field go straight across to the two gates in the opposite hedge and fence.

Here you rejoin the NWP by turning right and following the left hand fence. Crossing stiles and keeping the fence and then farm buildings on your left will bring you to a last stile onto the metalled lane at Caunsall.

Go left along the lane, crossing first the River Stour and then the Staffordshire and Worcestershire Canal, until arriving at the A449. Cross over this busy main road to the public footpath sign for 'Sugar Loaf Lane' and the fence stile next to it. Over the stile go forward to then walk diagonally left, across a ditch, to reach the top furthest corner where there is a double stile next to a wooden power pole. In the next field the path cuts the right corner by following the same line so reaching a step stile in the hedge ahead (85 degrees). Cross this stile into another field where you maintain the same line to a marker pole on the field crest. From the pole continue forward to the bottom corner where there is a fence stile taking you into another field at the bottom of a shallow valley. Walk up the valley bottom, keeping the fence on your left, until reaching the next stile which takes you into the wooded 'Fairy Glen' – no prizes for spotting one!

In the glen walk forward to merge with the bridleway that comes in from the right. Soon it becomes a nice hedged green lane and passes under overhead power lines. Reaching a point where there is a gated fence stile on the right and two gates to the left you now leave the NWP which continues forward. Instead you go left through the first of the two gates to now follow another bridleway by keeping the hedge and fence on your right. Heading towards the power lines you continue with the hedge/fence – passing through a gateway with a step stile and no fence – to the far top corner of the field where there is a wooden hunter's gate. Pass through the gate and turn left to the field corner where you then go right to follow the left hedge and fence. Ahead you can see Turbine Cottage immediately before which you meet a junction of tracks. Your way is directly forward up and along the unmade road that passes in front of the cottage. At the top of the rise, on the left, there is an area of grass verge where there is a gate left and two right. In the corner, on the left, there is a horse jump which you cross to enter a field.

In the field your way across it is diagonally left, aiming for a point well left of a large tree in the hedge (305 degrees). On this line, as you approach the hedge, you will see a gateway; walk to it. Pass through the gateway into another field and turn immediately right through a gap, between the gate and a water trough, into the corner of another field. Here your line is diagonally left again, aiming for the right hand edge of the barns ahead (305 degrees). This line in turn brings you to a step stile in a fence which you cross into another field. Continuing the same line; whilst negotiating a pool and tractor tracks; aim right of the large tree which is right of the barns. This will bring you to a gate with an old step stile at the side and so onto a surfaced lane.

Go left along the lane and follow it to the A449 where you now turn right to walk past the Whittington Inn to its second car park where a public footpath sign for 'Lower Whittington' points left.

Steeped in history; the Whittington Inn was formerly a manor house built in the fourteenth century by Sir William de Whittington, grandfather of the famous Dick. Since those days it has seen many reputed comings and goings, including those of Lady Jane Grey and also King Charles II as he fled from the Battle of Worcester – though, since it is documented that Charles passed through

Stourbridge and then arrived at Whiteladies at three o'clock in the morning, I feel this latter visitation is rather unlikely. However, it is worth a look inside the inn if only to discover its full and remarkable history.

At the sign for Lower Whittington walk left across the car park where a waymark directs you onto a grassy path. Following the path, which soon becomes hedged on both sides, takes you down to emerge in front of 'Willow Cottage'. To your right are wooden posts, one of which is waymarked with a public footpath sign. Go between them and in a few yards arrive at a gate. Here you are spoilt for choice, for apart from the gate itself there is also a step stile and a kissing gate! So, going through or over, enter a field and walk to the canal side where you now follow the field bottom and the canal to another kissing gate in front of woodland.

Entering the woodland you now follow a delightful path which brings you to, and through, a small wooden wicket gate into a garden. Do not be put off for it is still your right of way which now passes in front of cottages on a clear and well trodden path. *Now the unusual and beautiful views hereabout begin to unfold; not for nothing is this area called Gibraltar Rock!*

After the cottages you will pass a gate with a sign stating 'No public right of way, danger subsidence, path closed'. This is no problem for your right of way goes just right of this gate on a clear path which rises until enclosed on both sides. *You are now on a terraceway above the River Stour and the Staffordshire and Worcestershire Canal which can be seen left and below.* Stay with the enclosed path to exit through a white gate.

Now turn left down a waymarked path at the side of a house. This brings you to an unsurfaced road at a white cottage with a double garage. Go right along this narrow road and follow it to its junction with the road at Dunsley – notice the name plate at the junction. Now turn left and follow the road across the canal and River Stour to return to the High Street in Kinver.

Pied wagtail

10
Iron Age to Iron Horse
Craven Arms

From its position as a natural demarcation point between rolling Shropshire and the Welsh Marches, plus its obvious position at an important crossroads; one could be forgiven for thinking that Craven Arms would have a long and possibly turbulent history. Nothing could be further from the truth however for in fact this small market town owes its short existence to the coming of the railways during the last century – it even owes its name to an inn that predates it.

Nonetheless, despite its unpretentious origins, it does provide a very convenient starting point for this pleasant Shropshire walk that follows a line above the Onny Valley and then visits a most impressive Iron Age Hill Fort.

DISTANCE: 9½ miles
MAPS: Landranger (1:50,000) 137. Pathfinder (1:25,000) 931 & 951.
PARKING: Public Car Park in Craven Arms
PUBLIC TRANSPORT: British Rail to Craven Arms, or Midland Red West service 435 (Ludlow-Craven Arms-Shrewsbury)
START/FINISH: Craven Arms (GR 433828)

FROM the B4368 in the centre of Craven Arms turn along Market Street and follow it to a school and the Stokesay Castle Hotel at its end. Here go left and then right along 'Newton' to follow it to a point where the tarmac swings left and brings you to a white, metal and gated footbridge over the River Onny.

In a field on the other side go right with the river bank to then quickly veer away from it so as to find a footbridge over a tributary stream which is just in front of a high embankment. Over the footbridge follow the clear path up the side of the embankment to join a barbed wire fence which, keeping it on your right, you follow into the field corner. *This embankment has formed a natural barrier to the river and it is interesting to see how the Onny has had to twist sharply to avoid it.*

In the field corner is a fence stile that you cross onto a path at the very edge of the embankment. Continuing forward with the edge (right) and a fence (left) will shortly bring you to a step stile that you cross into a field where you maintain your line now with the fence and river on your right. Having gradually descended with the field edge you now meet the river again and follow its bank to a fence stile and then a field corner immediately before Stokesay Bridge.

On the way you will notice a marshy section left of the riverside path and in wet weather it is advisable to go left around this to reach the stile.

Having arrived at the field corner just before the bridge – which takes the A49(T) across the river – just a few yards to your left you will see a step stile and steps up the low embankment of the old A49 road. Walk left to the step stile but do NOT cross it, instead, with your back to the stile, strike across the field – almost back on yourself – to the protruding corner of the fence a few yards distant. At the corner go forward with the fence to an electricity pylon where you now veer slightly right across the field to the topmost corner where there is a gate. Here cross the fence stile into a lane that you follow left for about 80 yards to a public footpath sign on the right.

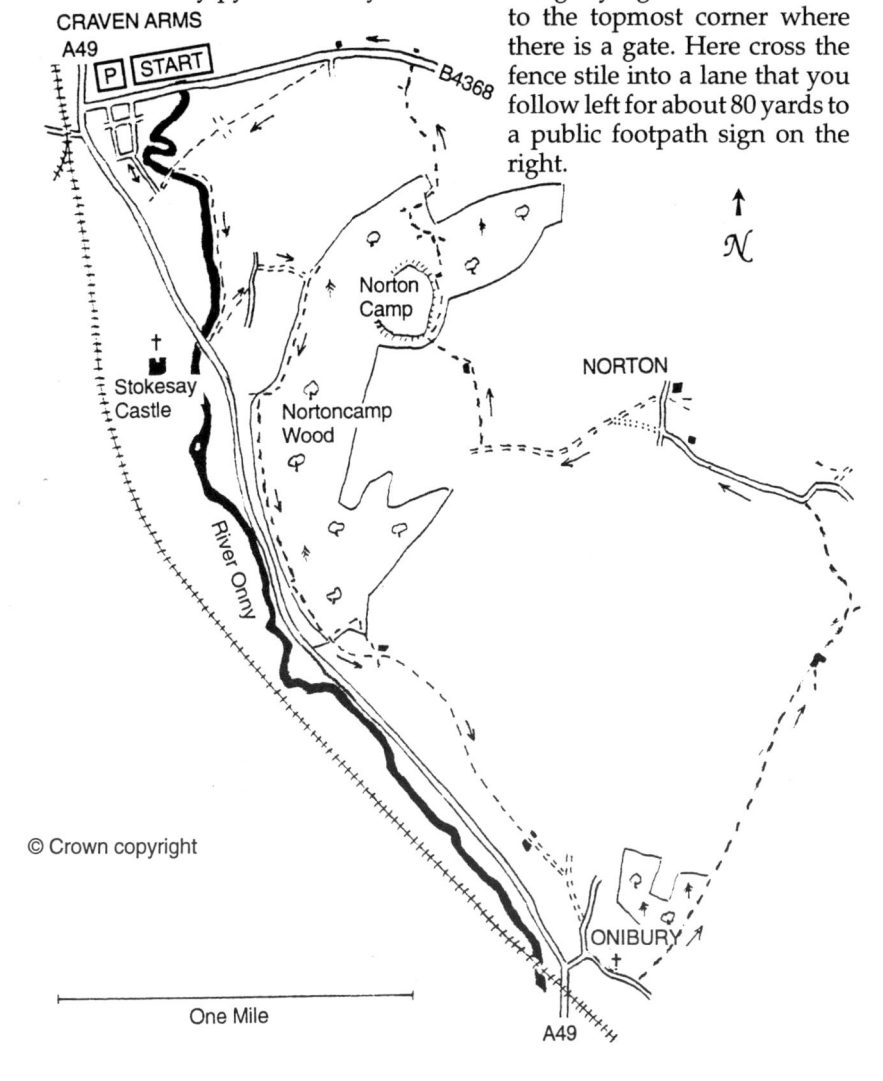

Turning right with the sign, follow the enclosed path up to a point just before the woodland – and just after a marker post indicating left – where the path splits. At the split, although the primary path is left, your path is the right fork. So go right with it into the woodland edge where it swings right to follow a line near the bottom edge of the trees. You now follow this clear path/track for about a mile.

On the way you will pass a gate and stile on the right that offers nice views across the Onny valley to Stokesay Castle and church. Stokesay Castle is a well preserved, fortified manor house dating from the thirteenth century and was built by Laurence of Ludlow, a wealthy local wool merchant. The gatehouse dates from Elizabethan times.

The castle is now in the care of English Heritage and, if you have time after the walk, is well worth a visit.

Having followed the track for the mile you will begin to approach habitation! The first house you will see is a few yards right through the trees, soon followed, in the garden, by a black corrugated and barrel roofed shed. Just past the house and garden you will see a marker post (which can be a little misleading) where you go right and down the short distance to the broad track below.

At the track go left – on a parallel line to that followed before – to pass left of superior pigeon lofts, and then a house, to arrive at a junction where the main track goes left and up while to the right a grassy hedged green lane descends. *There is a waymark post at the junction but it can sometimes be overgrown.* Go right down this hedged bridleway and in a short distance emerge at the gate to 'Keepers Cottage'.

Here go forward to cross a drive and pass between a house (right) and small white cottages (further left) where, ignoring the track bearing left into the woodland, you continue straight ahead and up the part tarmac track. Just inside this track is a large oak tree and next to it a green letter box. Only ten yards past the letter box the track swings left. Here, on the right of the bend and up, there is a fence stile in the recessed corner which is only just visible. Leaving the track climb up to the stile and cross it into a field.

Now in the field go forward with the right hand hedge to the next corner where there is a gate, a fence stile and a public footpath sign in front of a stone barn. Here cross the stile to join a bridleway and go immediately right through a hunter's gate. Walk forward to the barn corner and a crossing farm track to turn left through a gate where you follow the track as it swings right and then starts to swing left between two metal open barns. Here leave the farm track by going right to pass close to the right hand barn and so pass through a gate into a large field where you face a long field crossing.

At the time of writing the line of the bridleway across the field and through the crops had been restored thus making navigation simple. Should this not be the case in subsequent years then the way is directly across, heading for a hunter's gate in the opposite hedge and on a line left of a tree in the centre of the following field.

Crossing the field and arriving at the gate go through into the next field and so through the gate in the opposite fence. Now in another field go forward across the slope, rising slightly left, to meet the top left hedge. At the hedge go forward with it on your left to farm buildings where you then go through a gate to pass between the buildings and so swing a little left and then right into a hedged and unsurfaced lane.

Now following the lane pass through a gate and continue down it to pass a cattle grid and bungalow on the right after which your lane becomes surfaced and swings right, descending to pass a stone house with the year 1871 and the initials DA carved above its porch. This brings you to a T-junction where you turn right into Onibury passing thatched cottages to arrive at another T-junction. Here you turn left, signed for Walton, to pass Onibury church.

At this second T-junction a diversion right to the old Onibury Station Tea Rooms is recommended where a full range of refreshments – plus accommodation – is available, all reasonably priced.

Continuing your walk past the church, and just before the last houses on the right, you will come to a public footpath sign on the left. Go left with it up a hedged green lane to a point where the right hand hedge gives way to a fence and the lane bears left to a gate. On the right hand side of the bend there is a gated step stile in the fence that you cross. In the field you turn left to walk up the edge with the fence and woodland on your left. In the top corner you cross another step stile into another field where you follow its edge up to the next corner. Here there is a waymarked step stile that you cross to again walk forward with the hedge on your left. In the next corner is yet another step stile over which you are now faced with two centre field crossings. So, maintaining the same line, walk across the first field to the waymarked step stile you can see in the hedge opposite. In the next field cross it by maintaining the same line forward and so arrive at a bridged ditch and waymarked gate in the opposite hedge near to a metal water trough.

Over the ditch and through the gate go half right to cross another footbridge and so pick up the right hand hedge. Go forward and up with this right hand hedge where in a short way you will meet a step stile in it. Cross over into the adjacent field and go half left to cut the field corner to another step stile. Over this walk half right, aiming for farm buildings, to yet another step stile in the opposite hedge. In the next field walk towards barns and joining a track cross a gated step stile to pass between the barns to another gate into a field. Passing an 'antique' corrugated shed on cast iron wheels, continue forward with the right hedge to another gate. Through this go forward on a short, grassy track to pass through the gate a few yards ahead. Continue along the track now with a hedge (left) and a fence (right) to another gate and fence stile. Crossing into the next field follow the left hedge to another gate and fence stile over which you stay with the same line, still with the hedge on your left. At the next gate go through and past a pool to another gate a few yards ahead that gives access to a surfaced lane at a bend.

Turn left along this lane to follow it, passing a large stone house, all the way to its junction with a tarmac road where opposite is an unsurfaced lane.

To follow the right of way requires a right turn along the road (signed Craven Arms) for 100 yards to a bridleway sign on the left just before farm buildings on the right. This bridleway is enclosed and largely overgrown and while one or two hardy people have negotiated it there are several obstructions – not least being the remains of a pheasant rearing pen – before the unsurfaced lane you saw earlier joins it on a bend, thus merging with the right of way – see the sketch map. Consequently the practical solution to avoid these obstacles is to proceed as follows:

At the junction with the tarmac road, cross directly over to the unsurfaced lane opposite and follow it for 200 yards to the point where it bends left and where the line of the right of way joins it from the right. Stay with the lane around the left bend – now hedged on both sides – and follow it for about another half mile until it enters a field near two sets of double gates where you are now left with just the right hand hedge. Continue forward for 75 yards when you will come to a gated step stile in this right hand hedge and where there is a sign stating 'Footpath Only'. Turn right and follow the clear track up the edge of the field to a slight left bend with a small stand of trees on the left – formerly Camp Barn. Stay with the track around the slight bend to follow the right fence and soon enter trees at a brick barn with derelict houses left.

Straight ahead – past the barn, through the dyke embankment, and about 25 yards off the right of way – is the huge inner circle of Norton Camp Iron Age hill fort. The size of the circle suggests that the site was of some considerable importance and, judging from its position, was probably the guardian of the important cross-roads in the vicinity of Craven Arms – there is the line of a Roman Road just over two miles west, another Watling Street! About seven miles to the south-east is another Iron Age hill fortification, Caynham Fort, and the likelihood is that both of these positions formed part of a chain of interconnected signal stations.

Just before the brick barn your right of way goes right along the bottom of the outer ditch, with the rhododendron covered embankment to your left and a field hedge up to your right. Follow this clear path as it imperceptibly moves away from the ditch and dyke, passes a water tap, and then arrives at a marker post. *From here there are several diverging paths so take care and time.*

At the marker post the primary track goes left but you go forward, now leaving the fort behind, to descend a lovely grassy path through the trees. Arriving at another marker post continue with your track as it swings left and descends. This will bring you to another marker post indicating paths left and straight ahead. Here you continue forward when in a mere 20 yards there is yet another marker post where you go right, to leave the primary path, and follow a less frequented path down to a double stile on the edge of the woodland.

Crossing into a field go left along the edge with the woodland fence to its protruding corner. *Now you have good views along and up the beautiful Corve Dale.* Here turn left with the fence to a step stile in the inverted corner. Crossing into a steeply sloping field go diagonally right down and across the field to a gated step stile in the lower corner – on the way you will pass immediately left of a very small, shallow and disused quarry (little more than a depression!) in the middle of the field.

In the next field go forward and left with the left-hand hedge and fence. At the next corner, just right of a gate, cross a broken step stile where the path now splits – one going straight ahead towards a cottage and the road, the other going half left. Yours is the one straight ahead across the field to the cottage and the B4368 road.

Turn left along the B4368 in a while passing a side road on the left and then immediately arriving at a broken footpath sign, also on the left, near to a telegraph pole. Cross this left step stile into a field and walk half right (240 degrees) to proceed parallel with the stream a few yards to your left. This line will bring you to a bottom field corner and a step stile into a large field.

Directly opposite and across the large field you will see the white, metal and gated footbridge that you crossed at the beginning of your walk. Make your way forward, cross the footbridge and return to Craven Arms.

Crab Apple blossom

11
England's Kitchen Garden
Little Witley

The western parts of Worcestershire in particular boast some delightful countryside with rolling, tree topped hills all around. This fertile part of the county is such a rich mix of fruit and veg. that whoever named Kent 'The Garden of England' had never visited Worcestershire!

The walk description starts at Little Witley a small village not far from Witley Court.

> DISTANCE: 9½ miles, 6 miles, or 5¼ miles
> MAPS: Landranger (1:50,000) 138. Pathfinder (1:25,000) 973 & 974.
> PARKING: Roadside Little Witley OR Hampstall Inn car park, Astley Burf (GR 813679) – at the time of writing a modest fee of 50p is payable by non-patrons but free if you imbibe. If several cars are involved then prior permission should be obtained. Tel: 0299 822600. Meals are available.
> START/FINISH: Little Witley Church (GR 783635) for 9½ and 5¼ mile options *or* Hampstall Inn (GR 813679) for 9½ and 6 mile options (see page 53) *or* where convenient on the circuits.

Facing St. Michael's Church lych gate, Little Witley, take the enclosed footpath on the right and follow it to a tarmac lane. Here turn right with the lane until reaching the junction with the A443. Go left and follow the pavement for about 300 yards when on the right you will see a public bridleway sign at an unsurfaced farm road, next to 'Primrose Bungalow'. Go right to follow the farm road as it descends to cross Shrawley Brook and then rises to arrive in front of Dingle Farm. Here your track swings right and left to take you right of the farm and buildings beyond which you will meet a metalled road.

Cross the road to continue the same line on the broad unsurfaced bridleway almost opposite. After a while, at an old railway wagon and power pole, your clear track starts to swing left and takes you down between two stands of conifers to a pool. Passing left of the pool continue forward to the fence gate in front of you.

Now two field crossings follow which only present a difficulty if they have just been ploughed. The route is in fact well used by riders and walkers alike and is usually marked by small white marker sticks. The line on the map is a direct one (20 degrees) but at the time of writing – at least on the ground – it was slightly different so it is now described.

England's Kitchen Garden 49

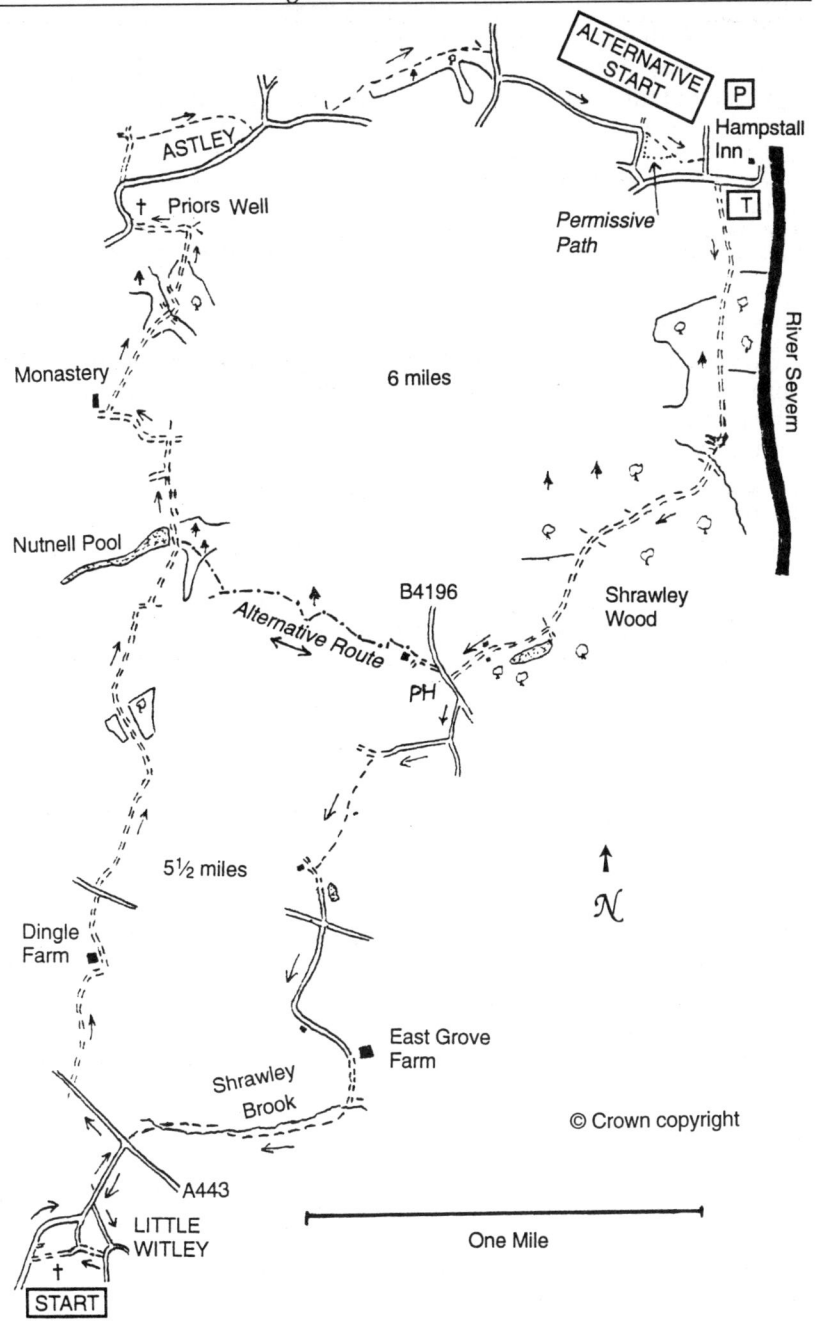

ALTERNATIVE START
P
Hampstall Inn
T
ASTLEY
† Priors Well
Permissive Path
River Severn
Monastery
6 miles
Nutnell Pool
B4196
Shrawley Wood
Alternative Route
PH
5½ miles
Dingle Farm
East Grove Farm
Shrawley Brook
N
© Crown copyright
A443
LITTLE WITLEY
START
One Mile

Go through the gate and in the field go forward for about 100 yards when the way swings right to pass under power lines and aim for the right-hand of three oak trees. This line will bring you to a metal hunter's gate in a protruding corner of a fence. Passing through the gate go forward the few yards to the next corner where you now cross this field diagonally left (30 degrees) to the far left corner and conifer trees. Entering the trees the bridleway takes you to the corner of Nutnell Pool.

If you are walking the 9½ mile route then follow the directions from ➤➤ *below.*

> *If you are walking the shorter 5½ mile route then this is your demarcation point. Read on...*
>
> At the corner of Nutnell Pool turn right along the broad track through the trees. Follow it as it rises and then descends to another, but much smaller, pool. Pass left of the pool to enter a sloping field at a gap and fence stile.
>
> In the field go very slightly left and up (155 degrees) to a step stile in the top left corner – it is possible to follow the left perimeter if the way is cropped. Cross the stile and walk forward along the top edge of a field with the embankment hedge and fence right. This will bring you to a gate in front of trees. Go through the gate and follow the trees the short distance to the protruding corner of the woodland. Here turn left and still with the trees, and then a hedge, on your left follow the field edge to a gate in the corner.
>
> Go through the gate and cross the field, slightly left, to the protruding hedge corner well below the farm buildings – 95 degrees. At the hedge corner walk forward the few yards to the galvanised water trough in the inverted corner. Cross the step stile at the side and continue forward with the remains of a hedge on your left – passing an isolated step stile on the way – to reach the next corner in front of a static caravan site.
>
> Here go all the way into the corner where you will see a broken step stile that takes you left and right down an enclosed footpath between caravans. This will bring you down to pass left of a house and onto the unsurfaced site road. Continue forward and down to leave the site through a gate and so reach the B4196. Turn right along the B4196 to pass the Rose and Crown pub.
>
> *Now continue from (✳) on page 55.*

➤➤ Cross the dammed head of Nutnell Pool and on the other side join a gated crossing track. Go right through the gate and walk the few yards to the field corner. Here swing left to follow the right hand hedge up the field to the top corner. Here swing left again for 30 yards to a gate on the right. Pass through this straight onto an unsurfaced crossing track.

Turn right along the unsurfaced track when shortly you will come to a T-junction with another unsurfaced track. Here go left to follow the track to a point approximately 75 yards before the entrance to Glasshampton Monastery where, on the right, there is a gate and metal hunter's gate in the fence. Your way is through the hunter's gate.

From a distance the monastery looks rather like a grandiose stable block which is not surprising for that is precisely what it was. It belonged to a large mansion house in the adjacent field which, not long after it was built, burnt down during the second decade of the nineteenth century: the stable block was converted in 1918 and in 1947 was occupied by the Society of St. Francis, an Anglican Order, who occupy it today.

Before continuing, do walk up to a point just in front of the monastery entrance – you are still on a right of way – to read the inscription beneath the clock tower 'There stood by the cross of Jesus his Mother'.

Go through the metal hunter's gate and forward across the centre of the field on a just distinguishable grassy track, heading for the protruding tongue of woodland ahead, a bearing of 30 degrees. Arriving at the fence

Looking across to Habberley Hill

around the trees go through the wooden hunter's gate and then forward and down a tiny, shallow valley to soon reach a T-junction with a crossing track. To your left is a wooden gate and to your right a metal gate. Here go right and just before the metal gate go left to cross the bridge over the stream.

On the other side follow the path as it swings left to follow the watercourse, upstream. In a short distance there is a junction in the path: one goes straight ahead with the general direction of the stream and the other goes sharp right along a lovely shallow valley. You take the right path to follow it up the valley and soon pass through a hunter's gate to continue along the well trodden, sunken track/path. This rises to a gateway into a field in which you go left to a gate. Go through to reach a surfaced track and so pass left of the church.

This is the parish church of Saint Peter, Astley. A handsome church dating from 1289 – there was an earlier church here at the the time of Domesday – the exterior fabric is sadly showing some decay. Inside are some excellently preserved Elizabethan effigies.

In the north aisle a rather poignant memorial shows a girl with an adder entwined around her arm. She was in fact bitten by the adder at nearby Glasshampton Hall and died as a result.

Just past the church the track brings you to a Y-junction with a metalled lane. Turn right and follow the lane a short way to a right bend. At the bend leave the lane to go straight ahead along the unsurfaced lane that is signed as a public footpath. In a short while your lane starts to bend a little left where there is a hedged green lane going off left. Just a few yards before this junction there are two hedge gaps on the right. Do not go through the first, larger one; instead go half right up a low embankment and through the smaller gap into a field. In the field go right, immediately passing a tree, and follow the right hand hedge.

After a short way you will see a step stile on the right that carries a crossing path. Ignore it to continue with the hedge to the next corner where there is a large gap. Go through and in the next field – which is usually cropped – continue your line forward across it (90 degrees – due east) aiming for the opposite hedge. About two thirds of the way across you will see a galvanised water trough where you alter your direction slightly by going half right (120 degrees) to reach a footpath sign at a hedge gap on a road. This is just left of farm buildings and right of a road junction.

On the road go left and then bear right at the junction to follow the sign for Astley Burf. In a while, on the right, you will pass the entrance to 'Pound Piece' just beyond which you will see a double public footpath sign on the left. Go left and, ignoring the step stile left, bear immediately right along the clear path that follows larch-lap fencing and the sign for Woodhampton. Almost at the end of this enclosed path you ignore a fence stile up on the right to walk forward to a step stile near a gate. Over this stile and into a field walk forward with the right hand fence and woodland edge. In the next corner cross a fence stile to continue the same line but now with the fence on your left. At the end of this fence there is a fence stile – which you ignore – where your path swings right. Go right with the path, through trees, to quickly arrive at the protruding corner of a barbed wire fence. Here maintain your line forward with the fence on your left and follow the path all the way to a step stile onto a road.

Turn right along the road and then left (signed Hampstall and Astley Burf) along Weather Lane. Follow Weather Lane for almost half a mile to a sharp right bend and a Royal Mail letter box set in a brick pillar. On the bend leave the road to continue forward the few yards with a public footpath sign (there is also a bridleway sign pointing left here) to a narrow gate in a chicken wire fence.

Here the right of way goes through the gate and into a field where you are faced with a hundred or more small rearing pens for game birds. While it is possible to weave your way through them – half right on a bearing of 125 degrees – and leave through another gate in the chicken wire, the farmer has provided a permissive route that is more convenient and is now described.

Instead of going through the fence gate go right to follow the outside of the fence to the corner. Here go left with the fence and after a little while you will be accompanied by a barbed wire fence on your right. Stay with the chicken wire fence until meeting the exiting narrow gate at a gorse bush. Here you are now back on the right of way where you go half right with the right hand barbed wire fence down a clear path. Soon reaching a gate and a crossing hedge your track swings left to gradually descend towards a corrugated iron shed just before which a path leads off right down steps to a public footpath sign on a tarmac lane.

On the lane go right and at a T-junction go left for a few yards where you then turn right along the signed public bridleway just before the telephone kiosk.

If you are starting your walk from the Hampstall Inn car park, then go back along the road and follow it as it bears right to pass houses and arrive at the telephone kiosk. Just after the kiosk go left along the signed bridleway.

Pass through the gate and follow the broad unsurfaced track that soon swings left into a farmyard. Do not follow it into the farmyard however, instead continue forward now on a narrower track that follows the edge of woodland for some distance and occasionally passes through gates. After one of the gates the track starts to swing right alongside wooden ranch fencing and along the bottom of a side valley. Here you leave the main track to go forward to the fence stile a few yards beyond the protruding corner of the ranch fencing. Over this continue forward to soon cross a footbridge over the stream coming down the side valley.

On the other side – in 10 yards – ignore a path going left to a gated step stile and a path going right through trees, parallel to the stream. Instead you continue forward and up through a shallow valley and the trees of Shrawley Wood.

Shrawley Wood is in the care of the Forestry Commission and is a designated Site of Special Scientific Interest. Tree harvesting has obviously been carried on here for very many years, as evidenced by the spindly coppiced trees you will see.

Arriving at a branch in the track take the left hand one and continue to rise to meet a broad grassy crossing track which you go over to continue your line. Soon you will see fields to your right as you now follow the woodland edge. This will bring you to a wooden sign which on the other side states 'Forestry Commission – Shrawley Wood'. Here there is a junction of paths/tracks where you continue forward, along the edge of the wood and with the fields on your right, to a gate and 'horse stile'. On the other side quickly pass through another gate – *to your left is an attractive woodland pool* – and follow the clear track alongside a right hand hedge. This will take you between houses and along a gravel drive to the B4196 opposite a pub, the Rose and Crown.

If you are walking the 9½ mile route then follow the directions from ➤ *on page 55.*

If you are walking the shorter 6 mile route based on the Hampstall Inn then the B4196 is your demarcation point. Read on...

Go right along the B4196 for a few yards and immediately past the white 'Pool Cottage' turn left along an unsurfaced road and through the gate for 'Caldecotts Caravans – Caldecott Farm'. Follow the road up to a partly timbered house where it swings left. Leave the road here to continue forward and up between a fence right and newly planted conifers left that takes you right of the house. Just beyond the house your way becomes an enclosed path that you follow up to a barbed wire fence where it turns left and follows it for the few yards to a stile.

Cross over to enter a field corner where you go right to follow the right hand hedge at the top of the field. Quickly passing an isolated step stile you will come to another step stile in a fence and next to a water trough. Over this continue forward with the right hand hedge and in a few yards meet its protruding corner. Here leave the hedge and go slightly left across the field (275 degrees – almost due west) to the gate in the opposite hedge at the lowest part of the field.

Go through into the next field and right, on your original line, with the ditch and right hedge. In a little while your right hedge becomes a woodland edge that you follow as it bears left to its protruding corner. At the corner go right, still with the woodland edge, for a few yards to a gate. Through this turn immediately left to follow the left hedge/fence at the top of a field. Arriving at a step stile cross over and go diagonally right (330 degrees) down and across the field to arrive at a fence stile and gap on the edge of woodland.

Go over the stile, or through the gap, to join a broad track and pass immediately right of a small pool. Follow the track as it swings left and rises through the trees away from the pool. This soon brings you to a T-junction with a crossing track immediately in front of the dammed head of a larger pool – Nutnell Pool – where you turn right.

Now continue from ➤➤ *on page 50 above.*

➤ Turn left along the B4196 (✳) when in a short distance you will come to a minor road on the right at Yew Tree Cottage. Go right to follow it as it rises and then at a Y-junction go right again to follow the signed 'no through road'. In a while and just after the last house – Grooms Cottage – the tarmac peters out and you are faced with three gates and a divergence of paths. The right hand gate leads to Goodyears Farm while the other two lead into fields.

Pass through the middle gate and in the field go left with the hedge on your left. *In the distance, and on the skyline, note the black and white timbered house which is soon your objective.* Arriving in the bottom corner of the field go through a gate into another field. Here go forward, slightly left, (195 degrees) to meet a line of oak trees where you go right to follow them to their end.

If this small section of field is under crops it is possible to go left along the edge for about 80 yards where, adjacent to the line of oaks right, there is a gate and step stile left bringing another public footpath in. Just go right to follow the line of trees.

At the end of the line of oak trees you have a field crossing where you aim for the left edge (220 degrees) of the black and white house that is now in sight again.

Arriving at the hedge in front of the house cross the step stile onto the drive where you turn left to follow the drive through a gate and onto a surfaced lane right of a pool. Follow the lane down to crossroads.

Go over the crossroads to follow the signed No Through Road for Eastgrove. Follow it for almost half a mile, passing Eastgrove Cottage Nurseries, all the way to East Grove Farm. At the farm pass right of it to follow a brick wall beyond which you go through a gateway to descend through a plantation. At the bottom, and just before the Shrawley Brook, the track swings left. You however go straight ahead to the footbridge over the stream.

On the other side go right along a charming little valley to follow the brook upstream. Shortly rise to a gate in a fence that crosses your path and through it continue forward and up with the right hand fence into a field. Continue along the field edge where, just before the next corner, you will see a step stile in the right fence. Crossing this takes you back into the trees high above the brook.

Now following the same line, but on the other side of the fence, continue forward to cross an up coming track until your path/track takes you down to another footbridge over the Shrawley Brook. On the opposite bank still follow the stream to cross a step stile in a fence, left of a gate. Stay with the stream to cross it again over a culvert bridge and so reach another step stile. Over this go forward and quickly meet yet another step stile. Beyond this you start to exit the valley by swinging left away from the stream and towards a section of fencing in the hedge up on the left. At the fence cross it by the public footpath sign onto the A443.

Across the A443 is a telephone kiosk and a junction with the road you used at the start of your walk. Cross to it and follow the sign for Little Witley. Arriving at a junction and signpost go left for Ockeridge. Shortly arriving at another junction go right for Ockeridge again. In only a few yards you will see an enclosed and gated footpath on the right. Enter it and follow it all the way to a narrow surfaced road on a bend. Turn left along the road to arrive back at the church lych gate.

Skylark

12
A Contrasting Circuit
The Malverns

Starting from a typically English village; following a bridleway across part of the Severn Plain; climbing the steep sided Malverns; descending stepped and gas-lit footpaths; following a low ridge that defies the surrounding flatlands; and finally walking through countryside that reflects its past connections with a large estate: all give this walk a special quality.

Situated approximately half-way between two important natural features – the Malvern Hills and the River Severn – Hanley Swan has a picture postcard quality: with a village green, a pub and a duck pond it has all the ingredients necessary to give it that quality. It is a fitting start to your walk.

DISTANCE: 9¾ miles
MAPS: Landranger (1:50,000) 150. Pathfinder (1:25,000) 1018 & 1019
PARKING: Roadside in Hanley Swan or Quarry Car Park and Picnic Area on the B4232. (If starting from the Quarry see box on page 60)
PUBLIC TRANSPORT: (Add 1 mile) British Rail to Colwall (see box on page 60).
START/FINISH: Hanley Swan (GR 813428) or where convenient.

FROM THE B4209 walk south along Welland Road – notice the old cider press on the left, set back from the road – and in about a third of a mile pass a school on the right. Just past the school, and on the same side, is a public bridleway sign for Malvern Wells – this is opposite the road for Gilbert's End. Turn right to follow the bridleway which is initially a roughly surfaced lane and soon pass Little Merebrook Farm. Ahead and in the distance you can see the broad, north/south sweep of the undulating Malvern Hills.

Suddenly the rough surfaced lane finishes in front of a large wooden workshop. Here you go forward through a gate and along the edge of a paddock, left of the workshop. At the end of the paddock go through a gate into a field and continue your line forward with a hedge and fence on your left. At the end of the field go through another gate and follow the same direction still with the hedge and fence left. Passing through a gate onto a farm road – to your left is Merebrook Farm – cross to the gate opposite and enter another field. Across the field you will see a field gate (left) a wooden hunter's gate (right) and between them an old tree in a

58   Ridges and Valleys III

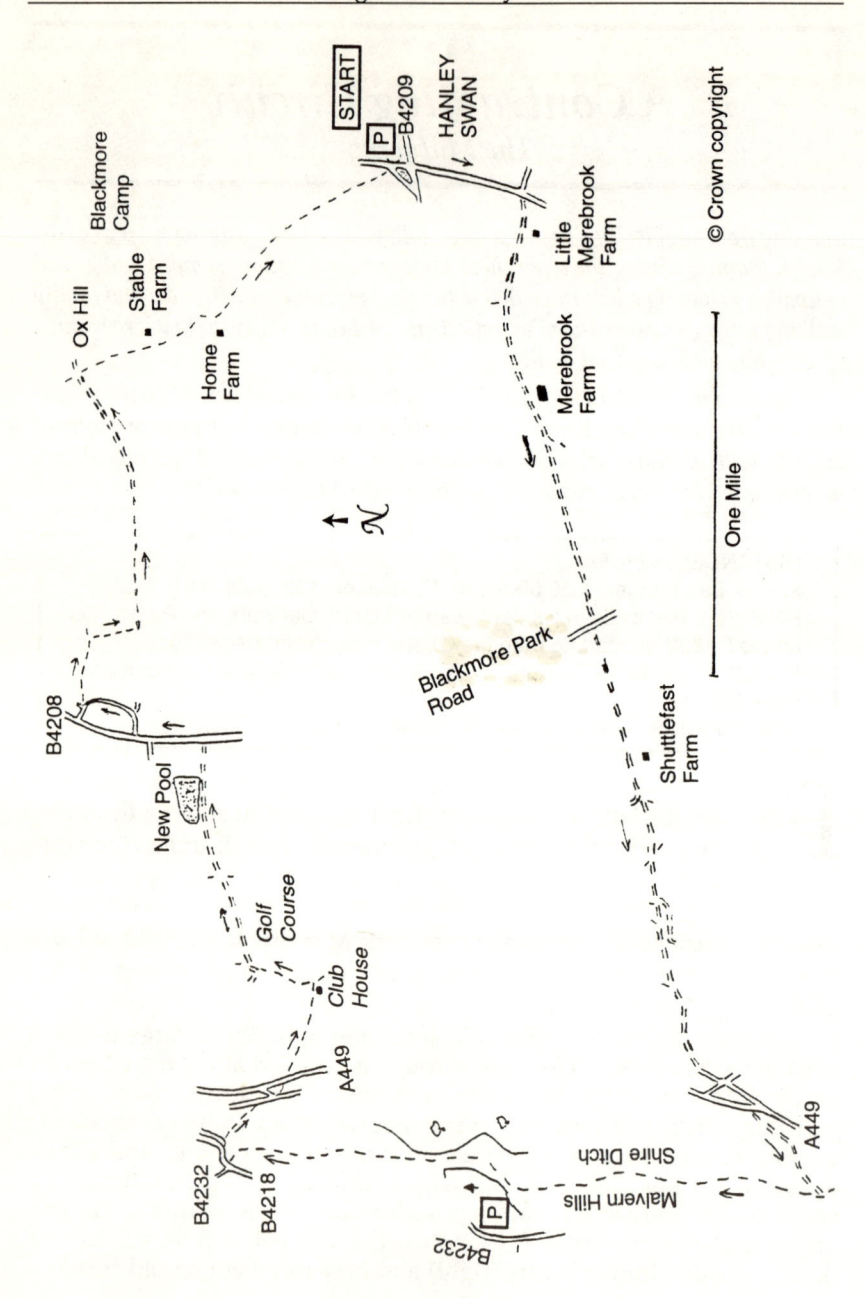

section of fencing. The gates denote a separation of ways – the left gate (signed) being a footpath and the right gate (yours) being a bridleway.

NB. *OS Pathfinder map 1019 has the status of the ways reversed at this point. However they are correctly shown on continuation sheet 1018.*

Cross the centre of the field to the hunter's gate right of the tree and so enter another field. Continue the same line, again with the hedge and fence on your left, that brings you to a metal hunter's gate in a crossing wooden fence. Go through and follow the hedge to the next corner and another hunter's gate – to your right are substantial new brick buildings. Go through this hunter's gate and over the sleeper footbridge to pass through the hunter's gate opposite. Still with the hedge and fence left walk along the edge of this large paddock and in the next corner go through a gate and then through another near a ramshackle building to meet Blackmore Park Road.

Cross the road and go forward along the signed bridleway right of 'Melbourne'. Quickly passing between two gates which bound the long dismantled railway line you enter a field. Follow the left hedge and line of telegraph poles all the way to the drive coming from Shuttlefast Farm. Join the drive to continue forward with it to the point where it turns sharp right. Leave the drive at the corner to go forward to the waymarked hunter's gate which is right of a step stile and field gate. Through the hunter's gate follow the left fence to a gate into another field. Again go forward; now with a ditch, hedge and fence left; to a point just before the next field corner. Here you will meet a marker post at a junction of bridleways and a footpath. Both of the bridleways go forward – *the left hand one goes through a wooden hunter's gate (adjacent to another gate) to pass a low concrete structure and follow a hedged and fenced track* – the right hand one (yours) continues forward, still in the same field and still with the ditch and hedge on your left, to the corner. Here go through the gate and follow the same line to the next corner.

In this corner there is a wooden hunter's gate between a field gate (left) and a fence stile (right). Pass through the hunter's gate and go forward along a fenced track with woodland on your right. In a short distance your track swings right and up to pass through a metal hunter's gate and so join a road.

At the road go forward to a 'Give Way' sign and letter box and so forward to a second 'Give Way' sign. Here go over the cross-roads and up Kings Road rising to a T-junction at the A449. Turn right along the main road for a few yards to then go left along Holy Well Road (leading to Holy Well) for about 25 yards. Here turn acutely left up a broad, unsurfaced track to quickly pass a Malvern Hills Conservators sign. *This is the start of a steep climb to the ridge top.*

Following the track upwards you will go over a crossing track to eventually meet the ridge top where there are several bench seats from which you can take in the surrounding vistas.

The Malvern Hills were formed 300 million years ago by a huge uplift in the earth's surface. Known as the Cheltenham Drive, this movement – geological rather than vehicular! – was responsible for throwing up a mixture of very old igneous and sedimentary rocks. Offering a superb panorama on all sides the hills are in the care of the Malvern Hills Conservators who protect them and look after the many paths that range over and around.

While there are paths that hug each side of the hills and are perhaps more comfortable during inclement weather, I much prefer the invigorating walk along the tops following the line of Shire Ditch – otherwise known as the Red Earl's Dyke – that marks the old county boundary. This ditch or dyke is now a much eroded shallow depression that follows the ridge top and is occasionally punctuated by a small boundary stone.

At the ridge top turn right to walk north along and over the high points.

Using Public Transport
From Colwall station cross the railway by the bridge and go straight forward into a field over a gate stile. Go half left and walk along the left hand edge of the field. Cross a stile into another field, go straight forward for a few yards, up the slope and take either of two paths that go right and into the trees. Reaching a field go up the bank ahead of you, heading towards the right-most of three trees. Cross a stile and walk forward with a hedge on your left and a row of trees on your right. Ignore a stile on your left, then swing right, keeping to the edge of the field. Cross a stile and take a track on the left leading through the trees. This will bring you to a café 'The Kettle Sings' which you go past to then swing right with a service road up to the B4232. Cross the road and take the broad track, right of the Quarry car park, up the hillside to the ridge top. At the top turn left to follow the main route.
Note the joining point so as to recognise it for your return journey.

Following the highest spots for almost two miles will bring you to a point where you descend steps to join the B4218, opposite its junction with the B4232. Here there are toilets, a bus shelter and a telephone kiosk.

Turn immediately right along the B4218 soon passing 'Worcestershire' and 'Malvern' signs where the road is cut through the hillside. Soon the road goes sharp left – here you go forward into 'Old Wyche Road' when you also turn sharp left, parallel to and just below the B4218. In about 15 yards you will see a public footpath sign on the right immediately before the white 'Fairview Cottage'.

Now begins a delightful descent through Upper Wyche, down stepped paths that retain their Victorian spa-town charm as well as their gas lamps. The first of these paths is known locally as 'The Pixie Path'!

Go right with the sign down a wide, steep path that is stepped for most of its length. At the bottom join a tarmac road where you go right to meet a T-junction. To your right are 'No Through Road' signs and opposite, what appears to be a small ornamental garden. Also opposite, and immediately left of the ornamental garden, is another enclosed path with a centre rail. This quickly takes you down to another road and lamppost immediately above the A449. Take the tiny footpath opposite down to the A449.

Cross the main road and go down the opposite tarmac drive, between 'Windscrest' left and the garage numbered 113 right. Quickly the drive starts to swing right where you leave it to cross the gated step stile in the left corner. In the sloping field follow the left fence to its protruding corner where you then strike out across the field, aiming for the large white golf clubhouse, to a gated step stile next to a large sign. Go over the step stile and forward to pass left of the clubhouse across its car park.

Arriving at a crossing service road in front of the flagpole, go left and follow it as it becomes unsurfaced and enters a strip of trees. Just a few yards in you will come to a junction where a track goes left at a white topped concrete marker post. Do not go left, instead continue forward through the trees for a further 50 yards where, immediately over a culverted stream, there is another white topped marker post. This directs you right, on a narrow track through the trees, to another white topped post on the edge of the golf course itself.

Here go slightly left across the course where ahead you can see another post in the distance. Head for it, on the way passing immediately right of a group of six silver birch trees, and on arrival continue forward on the same line to the woodland fence opposite where there is a white notice board and a wooden hunter's gate. Go through the gate to leave the golf course and immediately pass 'under' the dismantled railway bridge. Immediately 'through' the bridge you will come to a fence corner post with a profusion of waymark arrows. Here simply go straight ahead with a blue bridleway arrow along an enclosed track and accompanied by a brook. In a while your bridleway takes you right of the tree clad 'New Pool' and then, becoming a hedged green lane, delivers you to a road.

At the road (B4208) go left and follow it up to the edge of Malvern Common where the hedgerows disappear. From the gas lamp and road sign for Malvern Wells, continue along the B4208 for a further 75 yards where you go right along Hayes Bank Road to meet houses. At 'November Cottage' swing left with the road to pass in front of the houses to the last one – 'Wenlyn' – where the service road starts to swing back to the B4208. Immediately beyond 'Wenlyn' there is a public footpath sign pointing right along a rough surfaced lane.

Go right with the sign and in a short way come to the lane end in front of 'The Farthings'. To the right there is a step stile and a sign 'Dogs must

Old cider press at Hanley Swan

be kept on a lead' – the stile also bears the legend 'Tom Holland Walk'. Cross the stile into a narrow field and walk diagonally across to the far right corner where you cross a plank footbridge and a fence stile. In the next field go straight ahead to the fence stile in the opposite hedge at the bottom corner. Entering the third field do not go straight along the bottom edge, which is also a right of way, but go diagonally right across and up the field to the farmost top left corner. Here there is a step stile that takes you into another field where you go forward with the left hedge to cut a recessed corner and arrive at the next corner where there is a gate, topped with barbed wire, and next to it a fence stile.

Cross over and go forward with a hedge on your right where in about 30 yards you will see a step stile and old public footpath sign in the hedge. Over this stile go left to continue your line but now with the hedge and fence on your left. In the next corner cross a fence stile and maintaining the same line follow the field edge to a step stile in the next corner. In the next field continue forward to quickly enter a hedged track then, in a short distance, pass through woodland and then through a wooden hunter's gate onto a grassy area within a very broad hedged 'green lane'.

The 'green lane' is truly broad and spans the top of Ox Hill Ridge – Ox Hill being a corruption of Hawks' Hill, as it was called in Elizabethan days. This area was once part of a royal forest created by William the Conqueror and became known as Blackmore Park. When in the seventeenth century Samuel Pepys was re-building the Royal Navy this area supplied some of the timber for planking. Many of the surrounding farms, such as Stable Farm that you will soon pass, once belonged to the Park – which itself was part of Hanley Manor – and today still reflect that connection. The estate was finally broken up in the early part of this century.

Follow the track that meanders along the centre of the hedged area and after about a third of a mile you will come to a more grassy area with a solitary bench seat. To the left is a two step stile. About 10 yards further along and in the right hedge there is a plank footbridge and step stile.

Were it not for the bench seat it would be very easy indeed to walk straight past the two stiles – so be vigilant!

Cross the right hand footbridge and stile into a long narrow field. Walk the short distance forward across the centre of this field, crossing a 'gallop', to a step stile in a wooden fence. Over the stile descend a sloping field, with the hedge on your left, to join and go forward with a farm track. This takes you immediately left of drowning woodland and into a field where you walk up with the left hand fence to pass right of the farm buildings. Immediately past the farm buildings cross a gated step stile onto a roughly surfaced drive – to your left is the imposing Stable Farm with its clock tower.

Maintaining your same direction (almost south) follow the farm drive forward to soon cross a brick bridge and arrive at a junction where you bear left to pass left of Home Farm through two gates. Now stay with the farm drive which passes houses and then becomes a hedged lane before bringing you back to the green at Hanley Swan.

Seven-spot ladybird

13
A Midland Magnet
Bridgnorth

Bridgnorth has an alluring attraction for the inhabitants of the industrial Midlands which has endured for the best part of a century: understandably so, for not only has the town and surrounds many inducements it has always been relatively easy to get to.

Bridgnorth is an ancient market town on a sandstone ridge which dominates the historic River Severn crossing below. Not only does the town possess many historic buildings – including a church built by Telford; better known for his bridges and canals – the surrounding area has a plentiful supply of interesting features, some of which you will meet on this walk.

So let's leave the bustle and start the walk.

> DISTANCE: 10 miles
> MAPS: Landranger (1:50,000) 138. Pathfinder (1:25,000) 911
> PARKING: Public car parks in Bridgnorth
> PUBLIC TRANSPORT: Buses: Midland Red North service 890 from Wolverhampton. Trains: Severn Valley Railway (when operating) from Kidderminster.
> START/FINISH: The old road bridge over the River Severn (GR 719931)

LEAVE Bridgnorth by crossing the old bridge to the east bank of the River Severn. Turn left to follow the riverside path upstream when in a short while you will enter a public park. Just inside the park turn right at the finger post to then join the A442. At the road go left and then in just a few yards go right along the side road signed for the cemetery. Reaching the cemetery gates you will see to the left a public footpath sign and a flight of stone steps climbing an embankment. Take these steps to the top where you then cross a step stile and immediately turn right to follow a fenced path. In a short while the path swings left to follow the left fence and then reach a stile. To your left you begin to get a taste of the views in store. Cross the stile and continue upwards, now through trees, to reach the top of the escarpment where you will meet a field fence and a crossing path at the edge of the trees. *Note this point for your return journey!*

Now turn right along the crossing path and follow the top edge keeping the fence on your left. Soon you will pass the perimeter fence of a covered reservoir immediately after which you follow the main path to a point where it almost joins the track running from the reservoir. Here your path swings right with the tree covered edge to your right and a field to your left. Follow this path along the edge until it descends a short way to meet the A454 near the top of the notorious Hermitage Hill – the scene of many a trial and tribulation for cyclists and early-day motorists!

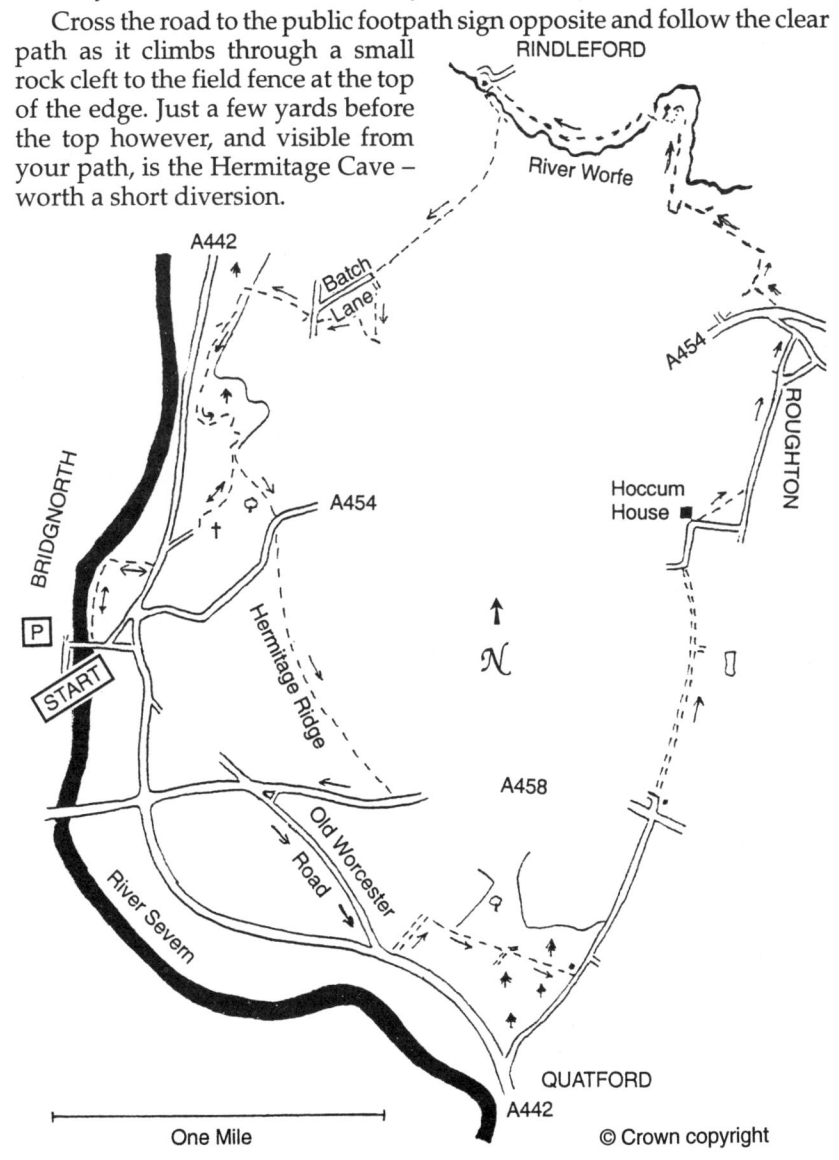

Cross the road to the public footpath sign opposite and follow the clear path as it climbs through a small rock cleft to the field fence at the top of the edge. Just a few yards before the top however, and visible from your path, is the Hermitage Cave – worth a short diversion.

One of the many man made caves in the sandstone ridges around Bridgnorth, this much eroded and initial carved cave is believed to have been the retreat of the tenth century hermit Ethelred, brother of King Athelstan.

At the field fence on the top of the edge turn right to follow the fence – keeping it on your left – along the top of the Hermitage Ridge. In a short while you will pass a second covered reservoir to continue on your path with the occasional view through the trees across the Severn Valley to the Clee Hills. After a while descend to the A458 where you turn right.

Now follows a period of road walking, unfortunate but well worth it in order to make possible this most attractive of circular walks.

Having turned right, follow the A458 down until almost at the traffic island. Just before you will see a sign directing you left along a short connecting road leading to the 'Old Worcester Road'. Follow it and at the Old Worcester Road go left again to pass various factory units before the road travels through green fields once more. In a while arrive at the A442 where, without quite joining the main road, you turn sharp left along an unsurfaced track which passes the attractive 'Fairacre' bungalow. Where the hedge and fence on both sides of the track ends – marked by the end of a line of scots pines – turn right along a fenced and hedged path. As the path begins to take you into woodland you will see the mock 'Quatford Castle' to your right.

Continue with the path, now with a wall on your right, as it progresses through the woodland and then descends to a shallow hollow where the right hand wall ends. Here take you time in choosing the correct route for it is easy to be drawn along the wrong way. At this point a clear track comes in from the right and in fact crosses your path, however, as it crosses your path it also swings right so as to initially follow the line of your direction – consequently it is easy to follow the track rather than your path. So, making sure you cross the track, now follow the discernible path that rises more steeply than the track. Soon you are much higher than the more obvious track below and you continue to climb when, a little further on, your path becomes sunken. After a while it brings you to the right of a house and a step stile onto a tarmac lane.

Go left along the lane and follow it for half a mile to meet the A458. *To your left is the Midland Motor Museum.* Go directly across the A458 into the 'No Through Road' signed 'Leading to Russell Close'. In just a few yards, at the unusual 'Stanmore Cottage', the tarmac road swings left whilst you continue straight ahead along an unsurfaced, hedged track.

To your right are nice views of the Morfe Ridge, whilst to your left is an area little recognisable as the former RAF Bridgnorth training camp – no doubt a place of great nostalgia for many a former National Serviceman!

Continuing forward with your track you will come to a wide junction where you maintain the same line to follow the left hand perimeter fence of some industrial units. Soon you leave these behind as your track becomes a truly grassy green lane and eventually meets a narrow tarmac lane at a bend. Go forward along the tarmac towards Hoccum House which is itself on a sharp right hand bend. In the corner of this second bend – next to a road sign warning of flooding – there is a public footpath sign which points through a gateway into a sloping field. Go through the gateway to join the field edge where you now cross the field to the bottom far left corner by aiming right of a wooden power pole in the field centre (60 degrees). At the corner, just above the lane, there is a large gap in the left hand hedge. Go through it and follow the bottom of this next field for about 10 yards when you will see another public footpath sign to the right and just below you. Descend to it and rejoin the lane where you go left.

Should you not wish to make this field crossing, you can always follow the lane to the same point – see the sketch map.

Now following the lane, which invariably has a substantial layer of sand on top of its tarmac; the result of water run off, you will pass a junction right and a footpath sign and stile left. Soon passing the attractive black and white timbered 'Willowbrook Cottage' you will arrive at a road. Here go left to then join the A454 which you need to cross. On the opposite side a metal gate automatically draws your attention but your point is right of this where there is a public footpath sign. At the sign descend steps to a step stile and in the field go a little left across the field to a step stile between two spindly trees in the opposite hedge (320 degrees). Over this second stile turn immediately right and follow the bottom of the field with the ditch and hedge to your right. Ahead you can see Davenport House sitting on its ridge. Reaching the field corner you will see another step stile in front, which you cross. Turning immediately left follow the field edge with the hedge on your left. Davenport House is now away to your right.

Stay with this hedge for the entire length of the field when you will arrive at a gate. Go through and follow the clear track forward as it then bends left towards a cottage. Now to your right you can see the River Worfe.

Ahead of you will be seen a gate between the corner of a brick barn (left) and the cottage garden fence (right). Go through this to the step stile just beyond. Over this, despite the direction of the arrow on the stile, go right along the path that passes behind the cottage. Following this attractive woodland path will soon bring you above the River Worfe and then down to a gate and step stile. Over the stile continue forward to follow a low rock face and stay with it as it turns a left corner. Around the corner you will see a wooden gate and step stile in front of a white house and its detached garage. Immediately left is a wide track that rises through trees – follow it as it swings round to join the half tarmacced drive and cattle grid in front of the house. Go forward with the drive to cross the bridge over the river and stay with it to reach a gate near a small white cottage where ahead you will see the bulk of the old Rindleford Mill.

Walk forward to the mill where, despite the various private signs, you turn left. Pass in front of the mill and through a fence gap – look out for the old mill wheel – and then cross two footbridges. Now follow the opposite bank of the Worfe upstream to the corner of a rock face on the right. Here there is a junction of paths, one going straight ahead to follow the river and yours going right through a gap between rock faces. Take the right path and follow this delightful grassy path as it gently rises up the valley known locally as The Batch. In a while your path merges with a track coming in from the left and so continues upwards to reach a gate just before a house and what I can only describe as a tiny brick 'Wendy house' – what would you call it?

Go through the gate and in front of the 'Wendy house' turn left along the track leading to a wooden gate with a 'Private' sign on it. At the gate go through the hedge gap on the right and follow a well trodden path as it swings left to follow the bottom of a shallow valley. This path takes you across a step stile and continues up the valley bottom to a point immediately before black corrugated iron sheds. Here you meet a crossing track immediately in front of a plantation where you turn acutely right to follow the track up to a gate in a hedge. Go through the gate and in the field walk straight ahead to the opposite fence and hedge where a marker post awaits you. At the post turn left and follow the fence to a gate through which you follow a drive forward to a minor road.

NB. At the 'Wendy house' it is possible to walk straight on up Batch Lane – see the sketch map – and so arrive at this same point; however the status of Batch Lane is unsure and the route described is more interesting.

At the road go right and immediately left into a green lane signed as a public footpath – ignoring a sign and step stile immediately on the left at the corner. Follow the green lane upwards to pass right of a cottage and then pass immediately right of the white cottage ahead. Now follow the hedged path forward and up to the top of the ridge overlooking the Severn Valley.

Here the path swings left to closely follow the top of the ridge with a fence to the left. As the path begins a shallow descent – but still at the top of the scarp – you arrive at a junction of paths. One goes right and down the escarpment whilst yours goes left and up to stay near the top of the ridge. Go left along this higher path and follow it up to the fence again. *This is a narrow, steep-sided path – known as Jacob's Ladder – where particular care is required when conditions are wet underfoot.* After a while you will arrive at a corner in the fence where it goes sharply left. You continue forward along the ridge on a clear path through the trees where after a while you will see a small, grassy clearing in front of you. Only a matter of a few yards before the clearing your path goes left and down to leave the path that has been worn to the clearing – remember this point.

By all means make the slight diversion to the clearing which sits atop a rock outcrop and provides a majestic, natural viewpoint. This is known as High Rock and gives outstanding views across Bridgnorth and the Severn Valley to the distant Clee Hills. Binoculars are a valuable accessory here. Retrace your steps for the few yards back to the main path

Continue with the main path to descend cut stone steps to a second outcrop and viewpoint. Here your path swings sharply left along a fairly wide path that initially contours the hillside. In a while you descend a little to cross just below the head of a small gully and then rise up to a crossing path at the top of the edge and next to a field fence. Turn right along the crossing path with the fence to your left and in a little while arrive at the path junction you noted not long after starting your walk. Taking the right fork, descend along the path of your outward journey and so reach the steps at the side of the cemetery.

Now it is a simple task to retrace your way back to the start of your walk and – if time allows – explore more of hidden Bridgnorth.

The Gaer Stone (Walk 14)

14
Faith, Hope and a Little Charity
Hope Bowdler

Hope Bowdler – 'Hope' being Old English for a blind (or side) valley; and 'Bowdler' being a later Norman family name – is today a tranquil and attractive village that belies its turbulent and violent past. The walk consists of two distinct phases; one of wild, open hills; the other of level pastures with panoramic borders. In each stage Hope Bowdler is the fulcrum and can be used as a base to form two shorter walks, each with its own attractions.

> DISTANCE: 10¼ miles, 5½ miles or 4¾ miles
> MAPS: Landranger (1:50,000) 137. Pathfinder (1:25,000) 910 & 931.
> PARKING: Lay-by on B4371 in Hope Bowdler (GR 474924) – see also page 74 (Acton Scott Historic Working Farm).
> PUBLIC TRANSPORT: British Rail to Church Stretton, or Midland Red West service 435 (Ludlow-Church Stretton-Shrewsbury) – add 1½ mile along B4371 to Hope Bowdler.
> START/FINISH: Hope Bowdler (GR 474924)

From the lay-by follow the B4371 eastward into the centre of Hope Bowdler where shortly, just past 'The Haven' and also on the left, you will see a public footpath sign and a step stile next to new houses. Over the stile follow the unsurfaced farm road as it quickly swings left and where you now leave it to go left in front of another house. Crossing the step stile between the house and the fence to the new houses, follow the enclosed path to another step stile to then continue forward and pass over a gated step stile. With a fence and stream left walk forward at the bottom of a steep pasture. Following a clear track pass through a gateway and then over a step stile to follow waymarked trees and a fence to another step stile. Over this go diagonally left across the field to pass immediately right of a power pole and meet a step stile onto the B4371.

Turn right along the road for 50 yards where there is a gate and farm road on the right leading to Gaerstone Farm. Go through the gate and follow the farm road to a point before the farm where there are two field gates on the right. Pass through the left hand of these and walk steeply up the pasture by following the right hand fence to the top corner. Here go through the hunter's gate to gain the open hillside where you immediately turn left to follow the intake fence. *Above and to your right is the prominent Gaer Stone outcrop.* Now stay with this clear path, which follows the fence

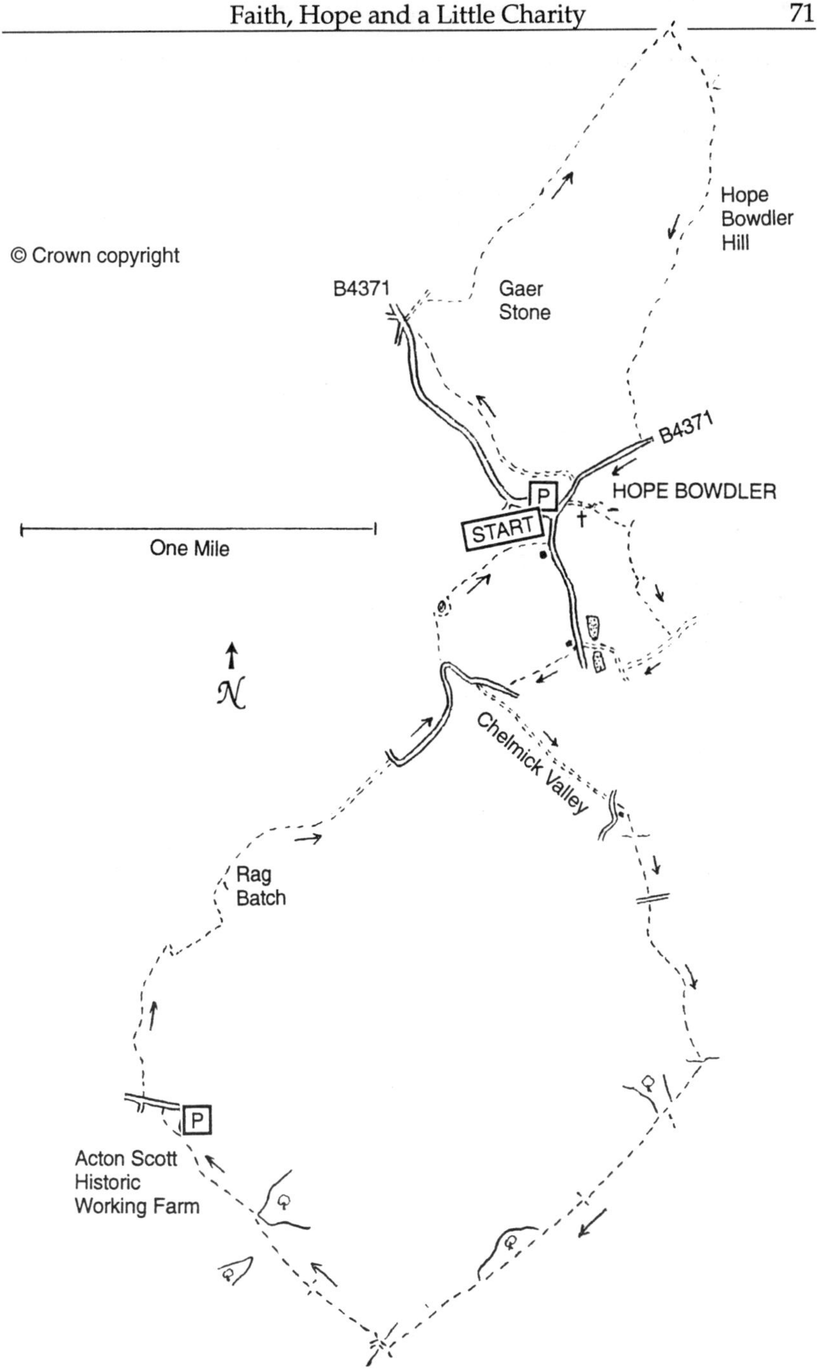

Faith, Hope and a Little Charity

© Crown copyright

B4371
Gaer Stone
Hope Bowdler Hill
B4371
HOPE BOWDLER
P
START

One Mile

↑ N

Chelmick Valley

Rag Batch

P
Acton Scott Historic Working Farm

and contours the base of the hill for almost a mile, until arriving at a waymarked hunter's gate in a fence.

In the distance and standing at 1506 feet are the man made ramparts of Caer Caradoc, an Iron Age hill fort reputedly the site of Caractacus' last stand against the Romans in AD50. Defeated and captured, Caractacus was taken to Rome where, because of the bravery he had exhibited, he was released and ended his days.

Caer Caradoc, together with the neighbouring Long Mynd, Ragleth, Lawley and Hope Bowdler Hills, belongs to the Pre-Cambrian geological era and comprises very hard rock covered with a thin layer of soil that supports little more than heather and bracken. There are some interesting Breccia outcrops.

Do not go through the gate, instead go acutely right up the clear path to leave the fence behind you. In a while your path meets a left hand hedge/fence and continues with it up the hill side.

Near the top of the saddle you will meet a junction of paths with a step stile in the left fence. You continue forward on the clear path that veers slightly to the right, away from the fence. After a fairly level section you begin a gradual descent to a gate where ahead you will see Hope Bowdler nestling in the valley.

Through the gate now follow the enclosed track down to another gate to then follow the left fence to a hunter's gate and so onto the B 4371.

On the road go right to arrive at the village notice board and red mail box. Here turn left along the unsurfaced road which passes left of the church to a junction in front of 'The Thatches'.

A diversion to look at the church is well worth the time. The lych gate is very old with stone roofing tiles and a large, carved block of stone beneath it where coffins were rested. This of course is the original purpose of a lych gate – 'a roofed gate to a churchyard, formerly used as a temporary shelter for the bier' – and is the only example of its practical use I have ever seen. The manor of Hope Bowdler dates from pre-Conquest times when it was held by a Saxon named Forthred and is recorded in Domesday Book as Fordritishope. It was one of the manors that once belonged to Edric Sauvage – the French name for a Saxon nobleman who conducted an armed resistance against the Normans who had dispossessed him, and who was known in legend as Wild Edric. It is not certain whether the Saxon manor contained a church but certainly by 1237 there was a Norman church here.

Shropshire County Council have devised a walking route named 'Wild Edric's Way'!

At the junction turn right to the gated step stile and immediately over this go left along an enclosed path to enter a small field via a hurdle gate. Following a well walked path to the gate gap ahead enter a sloping pasture. Here go forward and down with the left hedge to cross a footbridge and enter trees through a wicket gate.

Here you are at the bottom of Yelds Bank. Turn right and initially following the fence soon leave it at a junction to rise left on a steep path up the embankment. At the top, and on the edge of a field, go right for 20 yards to a marker post just before a protruding corner. From the post go left across the field (140 degrees) aiming for the oak tree, a telegraph pole and, behind them, a step stile. Cross the stile into a hedged green lane and turn right to follow it down past cottages to meet a crossing track at a T-junction. Here go right again and follow the track all the way to the tarmac road.

Directly opposite is the drive to Stonehouse Farm. Follow it to pass left of the house and at the rear walk forward and up with the left hedge to a gate. Through the gate continue with the hedge to another gate and so forward still with the hedge to the top corner where a fence stile takes you immediately left of a gate and down to the road.

Go right and down the road where just before the bottom and level with 'Chelmick House' you will see a signed bridleway on the left. Pass left through the gate and follow the broad fenced track that contours just above the valley bottom. Go through another gate and pass in front of a house to now follow the narrower, enclosed bridleway. This soon takes you past a cottage where you continue with your bridleway to eventually join a tarmac lane.

Opposite is a step stile next to double wooden gates. Cross it and walk forward with the hedge to the step stile ahead. Over this one go half right with the fence and hedge behind the cottage to cross a third step stile. Continue forward along the field edge to a fence over which there is a collapsed footbridge. Do not use the footbridge, instead simply step across the stream which is usually narrow enough to allow this. On the other side go up the bank to join the right hand hedge/fence and follow it all the way to the next corner where you cross a fence down to a lane.

Almost opposite, slightly right, is a gap and fence. Cross the fence into a field and go straight ahead to gradually meet the left hand hedge where there is a fence stile approximately half way along it. Entering another field go forward with the left hedge/fence – *ahead are fine views of the limestone Wenlock Edge* – to a gate in the next corner. Through this now go half right aiming for a broad section of fencing, an oak tree and a gate in the opposite hedge – due south. Passing through this second gate – left of the oak tree – go forward with the right hand hedge and follow it to a footbridge in the next corner.

Cross the footbridge into another field which you now cross diagonally right to the far right corner and the end of woodland. At the corner go through a gap and then immediately right for the few yards to another corner where there is a gate leaning against a fence around the woodland. Go through this gate, into the edge of the woodland, where you are now immediately faced with a path divergence. One path goes left to the corner of a field whilst the other, yours, goes forward along the edge and just inside the woodland. This fairly clear path will quickly bring you into the corner of another field where you continue forward with the left hand ditch, hedge and fence. In about 40 yards, across the ditch, you will see a gap in the hedge where the top strand of barbed wire has been cut. Cross the fence here and go right to follow your previous line now with the fence and hedge on your right.

Along this next section of path you will be able to enjoy the views of Wenlock Edge to your left and the Stretton Hills to your right.

Now you need to follow this right hand boundary for about a mile, crossing several fields on the way. Along the way – about two thirds of the mile – you will pass a woodland to your right. At the end of this woodland you cross a second step stile followed by a footbridge formed by a fallen tree – not at all as bad as it sounds! – to enter a large field. In the field continue following the right boundary to pass one step stile and then arrive at a second before the field end. Go right over this second stile and walk forward to cross a stone bridge.

Immediately over the bridge you will see a step stile to your right, cross it into a field. Here go a little left (310 degrees) to follow a line parallel to the left hedge up this long field. *Obviously former field boundaries have been removed for this field is almost half a mile in length!* As a navigational check along the way you will pass under a power line next to the second pole from the left, and then between two willow trees (one pollarded). Here adjust your line slightly more right (320 degrees) so as to aim well right of a stand of tall trees and a collapsed corrugated iron structure. This line should bring you to a step stile in the hedge/fence ahead, just above the corner.

Cross into another field and cut the corner by walking diagonally right across it (330 degrees) to a gate and fence stile at the corner of woodland. Over the fence stile follow the left fence up the field to a gated step stile in the next corner. On the other side walk the 10 yards to the protruding right fence corner and turn right with it and follow it up the edge of trees. At the top cross another step stile into a field where you go diagonally left – *the map shows the site of a Roman Villa in this field though there is no apparent sign of it* – to a gated step stile that takes you onto the car park and picnic area of Acton Scott Historic WorkingFarm.

Operated by Shropshire County Council this working farm offers a full and fascinating variety of country crafts as well as the opportunity to see how a living farm operated when shire horses were the real horse power. It is a useful place for a break with a café, picnic area and toilets.

With permission it is possible to park and start your walk from here though you should remember that the Farm is not open throughout the year or indeed every day; also the gates are closed at 5pm. If your party consists of several vehicles – especially during peak periods – then please make prior arrangements by telephone on 0694 781 306/7.

Leaving the car park by the main gate – or the step stile if the gates are closed – turn left along the road and follow it as far as the entrance to Acton Scott Farm. Opposite and on the right you will see a gate through which you enter a field. Cross the field on a definite track to arrive at the bottom left corner where there is a gate and step stile. On the other side leave the track to go right to a hunter's gate between two field gates. Through the hunter's gate follow the enclosed bridleway until it spills into a field where you now continue forward along the field boundary with the right hedge. Entering another field your bridleway becomes enclosed again and descends to pass through a hunter's gate, cross a footbridge and climb up the opposite bank onto the edge of a large field.

Here the line of the bridleway goes straight across the centre of the field. However a permissive route has been waymarked around the field boundary and as this seems mostly used it is now described.

At the edge of the field go right to the corner and turn left to follow the right hedge to the next corner. Here go left again to follow the bottom edge to a gate into the delightfully named Rag Batch. Go through the gate and then right with the fence to cross a culverted stream. A few yards on the other side you will see a hunter's gate right – ignore it. Instead stay with the broad rising track that takes you up to a gate and out of the trees into a sloping field. Walk forward with the hedge/fence on your right.

Now on the left you can enjoy even better views of the Stretton Hills while to the right and across Ape Dale, Wenlock Edge and the Clee Hills form a broad and impressive landscape.

After a while you will arrive at the next corner of this large field where a gate takes you into a hedged green lane. Follow the lane all the way to a gate and so onto the narrow tarmac road at Chelmick.

Here go right and follow the road as it quickly bends left. Soon it descends steeply to a right hand hairpin bend where you leave the road at two gates in the bend. Go through the left gate and follow the right hedge/fence as it bends right. Stay with it for about 250 yards when you will see a fence stile right, adjacent to a pool. Cross over and walk anti-clockwise around the pool to another fence stile below a steep bank. Over this walk the few yards forward to meet a left hand fence which you now follow forward to a corner with gates. In the corner go through the gate to continue your line on a clear track and with the fence now on your right. This will take you left of barns and a house to a gate onto a road. Go left along the road and so back to the B4371 in Hope Bowdler.

15
On Ditchford Bank
Hanbury

Without doubt one of the most impressive features of Hanbury Church is its position. A height of 330 feet may not seem much but is quite sufficient to allow commanding views over the surrounding countryside. This feature strongly supports the probability that the site was a fort in Roman times: having climbed the embankment you will certainly appreciate its defensive attributes! It has been a religious site since the ninth century when in 836 the Mercian King Wiglaf granted the land for a monastery.

Half way around this walk is Berrow Hill, another commanding viewpoint which, standing above the old Roman Road near Feckenham, lends credence to Hanbury's Roman associations. The whole of this area is within the former Forest of Feckenham.

About half a mile west of your finish in School Road is Hanbury Hall which dates from the early eighteenth century and is noted for its famous staircase and a fine collection of porcelain. Now in the care of the National Trust it is open to the public but only at certain times – telephone 0527 821214.

> DISTANCE: 10½ miles
> MAPS: Landranger (1:50,000) 150. Pathfinder (1:25,000) 974
> PARKING: Lay-by in School Road, Hanbury.
> START/FINISH: Lay-by, School Road (GR 955642)

FROM the lay-by in School Road walk the few yards to the public footpath sign immediately before the school. The sign points both left and right. To the right it indicates steps leading up to a step stile which you cross into a steeply sloping pasture. Walk straight up to meet a metal kissing gate which gives access into the church yard.

Here benches give you the opportunity to enjoy the magnificent views or simply recover your breath. When conditions are right the Malverns and Bredon Hill are clearly seen whilst further south the Cotswold escarpment is also visible. The church has seen many changes over the centuries one of which was the addition of an interesting Regency gallery which housed musicians and singers.

Leaving the church retrace your steps to School Road where you now turn left to follow the road for a little over 400 yards to a footpath sign on the left between the entrances to 'The Old Church House' and 'Rectory Gate Cottage'. Go left with the sign into an enclosed footpath which you

On Ditchford Bank

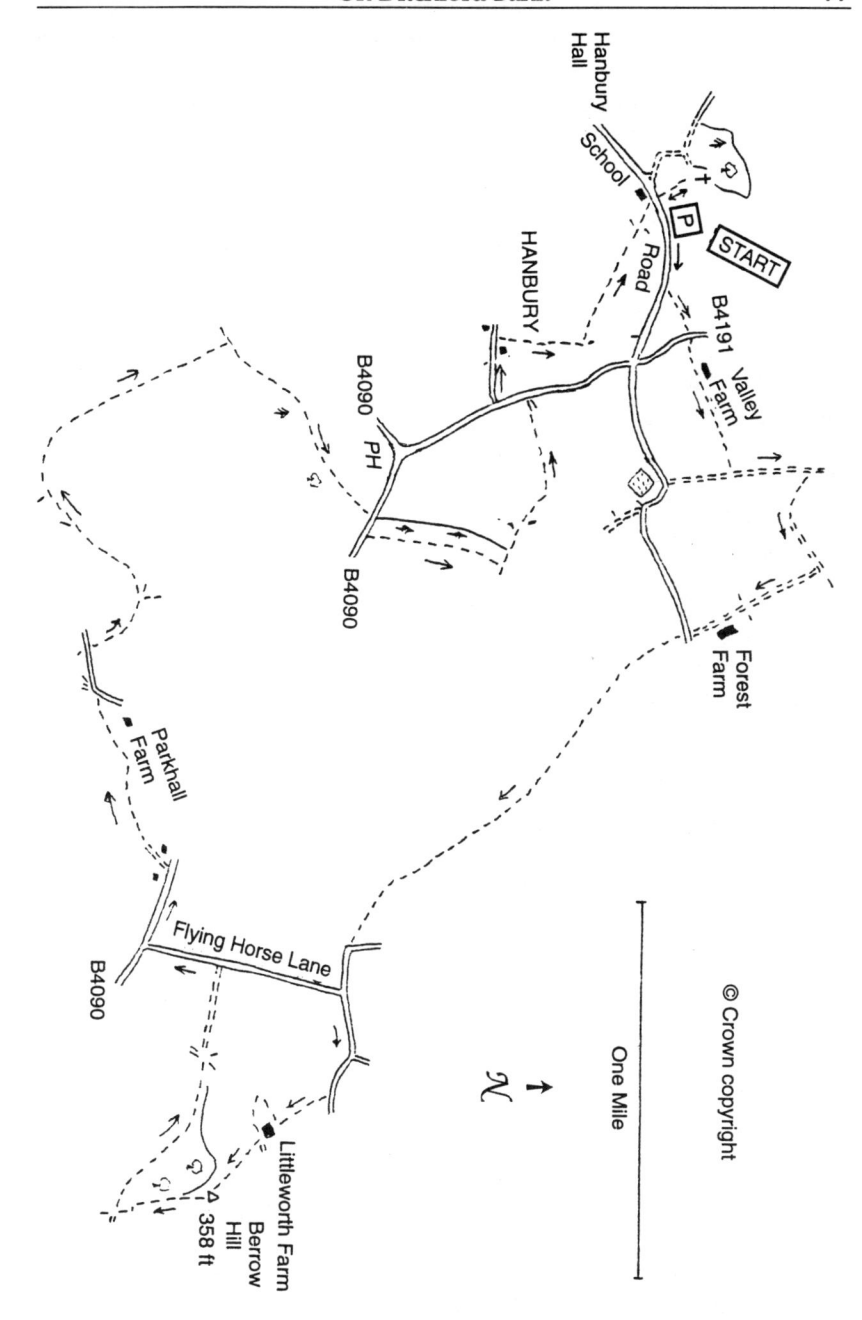

follow as it rises up a bank, passing through a kissing gate, to meet a gate onto the B4091.

On the other side of the road there is a sign for Valley Farm. Follow its tarmac drive as it swings down to pass left of a cottage and immediately right of Valley Farm itself. Immediately after Valley Farm the drive takes you in front of a thatched cottage where the tarmac ends. In front of you there is a gated step stile into a field which you enter. Go forward with the left hand hedge/fence and in the next corner cross another step stile. Maintain the same line in the next field when another corner stile takes you into a hedged green lane.

Turn left to follow the lane – *which can be muddy in places* – for approximately 500 yards when you will see a hurdle type fence on the left and, set back from the track, two successive gates on the right. Turn right through the gates, into a rough pasture with isolated trees, and go immediately right into the corner. Here go left and follow the hedge/fence, keeping it on your right, up the slope. This brings you to a gate next to an oak tree in the top corner through which you continue forward along the wide and enclosed gas pipeline route. In turn this soon brings you to another gate on the other side of which there is a crossing track. Go through the gate and onto the crossing track to then immediately turn right through another gate to now follow a broad avenue of oak trees. In a little while this takes you through gates, right of Forest Farm, onto a road.

Old stone cross near Hanbury church

Now begins almost a mile of panoramic walking along the rounded top of Ditchford Bank with superb views in virtually all directions. It's an unusual feature and a pleasant place to be.

Directly across the road are gates into another broad track. Follow this track as it leaves hedge and woodland behind and bears a little left now with fences on both sides – indeed the track/path now follows the centre of what is essentially a very long and narrow field. Soon passing a collapsing brick barn and then a pool continue to the end of this long field where, in the right corner, there is a gate which you go through to quickly reach another gate into a field.

In this field go forward with the left hedge/fence. Arriving at a second gate in the fence go through it and follow the same line but now with the fence on your right. In the bottom corner you will find a wooden hunter's gate which you pass through. Cross the concrete pipe that culverts a stream and follow the bridleway forward to quickly enter a field corner. Continue forward with the right hand hedge to reach a gap which takes you onto a tarmac road at a sharp bend.

At the road go forward (right) to the next corner – a Y-junction – where you now take the minor road forward (still east) to quickly pass a footpath sign. Stay with the tarmac as it passes Upper Berrow Farm, and then two bungalows, to reach the brick gateway to Littleworth Farm. Turn right through the gateway and cross the cattle grid to follow the tarmac drive all the way to a public footpath signpost immediately in front of another cattle grid in front of the house.

Here the right of way continues forward to pass immediately right of the house. However, the public footpath sign mentioned in the last sentence of the previous paragraph indicates a permissive route which avoids the house and this is now described.

Go right through the gate, next to the signpost, into a field and follow a left hand fence until arriving at a waymarked double step stile at the end of the garden. Now back on a right of way cross over into another field and then walk diagonally left (80 degrees) across the field to cut the corner and so arrive at a metal hunter's gate next to a water trough and well to the rear of Littleworth Farm.

Take your time here for your next path is not immediately apparent.

Do NOT go through the gate into the hedged track. Instead, at the water trough, go right to follow a barbed wire fence – keeping it on your left – along a rising, just discernable path that zig-zags through scrub woodland, bracken and undergrowth to soon reach a step stile onto the hill top pasture of Berrow Hill. Now simply walk forward to the triangulation pillar which stands at 358 feet.

Here again magnificent views await you on the sheep cropped summit – a good place to linger and well worth the effort of getting there.

From the pillar go half right to join the edge of the trees and follow them forward along the ridge, soon descending to a fence. Here turn right and walk down, close to the tree edge, to the bottom corner of the fence where there is a metal gate. Go through the gate and immediately right to follow the fence to the next field corner. Here go through the gate and follow the now enclosed track forward. In a while pass through a wooden hunter's gate, quickly followed by a metal one, to enter trees. Follow the clear bridleway – *with occasional mud patches during the 'rainy' season* – to soon reach a junction of paths and bridleways at an old bridleway sign for 'Berrow Hill' and 'Feckenham'.

At the junction continue straight ahead along a hedged green lane until reaching a tarmac road – Flying Horse Lane. Go left along the road to the T-junction with the B4090. Turn right along the B4090 and follow it to pass Bridge Farm on the right and then arrive at Brook Farm on the left. Immediately after Brook Farm, and also on the left, there is a gate and a signed fence stile. Cross it and follow the wide track until meeting two adjacent gates. Go through the right hand one and forward to pass into a second field through another gate. In this second field veer right to join the line of trees alongside a steam and so meet a gate. Turn right through the gate and cross over the bridged stream into another field. Now walk half left aiming for a point just left of farm buildings which will bring you to a gate left of Parkhall Farm. Through the gate continue forward to the far left corner of the next field where a gate takes you onto the bend in a road.

Walk forward (left) along the tarmac for about 200 yards when you will come to a step stile left and a fence stile right. Cross the right hand stile and walk forward and slightly left to a gap in the far left corner. Through the gap go forward with the remains of the left hedge to pass over a bridged stream. Immediately in front you will see a gate – ignore it. Instead go diagonally left to the far left corner of this field where you will meet a waymarked step stile.

Do NOT cross the stile but in front of it go left through a gap to follow the right hand fence. In a little while you will come to a step stile with a duckboard bridge which takes you over a wet area. This is immediately followed by a footbridge and step stile back into your original field. Resuming your forward progress continue following the right hand fence to the next corner where you go through a hunter's gate into a narrow field. Following the right edge as the field widens will eventually bring you to a corner. Here look out for a stiled footbridge which enables you to maintain the same line into a pasture.

In this pasture continue forward with the hedge/fence, still keeping it on your right, to follow it as it starts to loop right. In the second pasture you will eventually come to a low, but distinctive, crossing embankment which takes a footpath across your route. Here there are gates left and right. Go right through the waymarked gate and then immediately left to resume the same line but now with the hedge/fence on your left. At the end of this very long field cross the step stile in the corner and then the one a little way ahead in the following corner. Now turn right to follow the hedge/fence, keeping it on your right, to the top corner where there is another step stile. In the next field follow the same line and boundary to yet another step stile and so into another field where the same line will bring you to a final step stile onto the B4090.

To your left is the ivy covered Vernon Arms, parts of which date from Tudor times.

Go right along the B4090 for less than 100 yards where just before speed de-restriction signs there are steps on the left leading up to a step stile. Cross over into a field and walk forward with the hedge on your left for a distance of 40 yards when you will come to a stile and hunter's gate. Go over into trees and go right to follow the same line but now just inside the woodland. Follow the tree lined path all the way to the end of the woodlands where there is a step stile in the right corner which takes you into a sloping field. Here go left to follow the woodland edge and so arrive at a double stile in the bottom corner. Cross both into another field corner where just a few yards ahead is another waymarked step stile. Over this quickly pass through a narrow belt of trees and over another stile into a field. Here walk straight ahead along the edge of the field with the hedge on your left to the next corner. At the corner go left through a gap into yet another field where you face a centre field crossing.

Aiming for the far right corner – 270 degrees and a line roughly between the two sets of buildings in the distance – cross the field. At the corner is another gap which you pass through to then cross the next field – 250 degrees and aiming for farm buildings – which line will bring you to a gate onto the B4091.

Go left along the road and turn right along Pumphouse Lane. In slightly over 300 yards, and just before a house on the left, you will see a public footpath sign in the hedge on the right next to a tree and telegraph pole. Go right over its accompanying step stile and in the field go diagonally right to reach the far right corner. In the corner cross the fence stile left of the water trough and gates and in the next field follow the right hedge – left of houses – to the next corner and a step stile. This takes you into a small, young plantation where you continue your line along the right hedge to soon meet a crossing path with stiles right and left.

Cross the left fence stile to go forward and slightly right to a stile in the opposite hedge. In the next field continue the same line to a stile in the far right corner. Cross this and the next field, still on the same line, to two gateways. Go through both of these and in this last field walk forward to pass immediately right of the school to the field corner and School Road – the start of your journey.

16
Diddlebury Delights
Diddlebury

Diddlebury is another of those lovely Shropshire villages that straddle the B4368, Morville to Craven Arms road. With a stream and stone footbridge as the centre piece and a church that dates from Saxon times, it really is a picture postcard setting. As such it is an ideal place to start and end the description of this walk – which takes in Wenlock Edge and the beautiful Corfton Bache – though there are easier places to park along the route.

> DISTANCE: 11 miles
> MAPS: Landranger (1:50,000) 137. Pathfinder (1:25,000) 931
> PARKING: Limited roadside in Diddlebury (please consider locals and churchgoers). Small roadside lay-by at Corfton on B4368 (GR 495850). Car Park and Picnic Area at Harton Hollow near Upper Westhope (GR 480875).
> START/FINISH: Diddlebury (GR 507854) or where convenient *en route*.

As you approach Diddlebury church from the B4368 the village road goes left near a stream and stone footbridge. Next to the footbridge is a small wooden wicket gate and a public footpath sign. Go through the wicket gate and follow the watercourse downstream, crossing a stile, to a footbridge that takes you onto the opposite bank. On the other side walk up the slope to merge with the right hand fence and follow it to the step stile in the top corner.

Now in parkland pasture, with splendid tree specimens around, go directly forward in a south-westerly direction (215 degrees) to cross a surfaced, unfenced track. Maintaining the same line, well left of a gap and gate in the opposite hedge, will bring you to a smaller gap containing a step stile. This takes you into a field where you continue forward now with a hedge on your left.

Just before the end of this large field you will come to a gated step stile in the left hedge which you now cross. Immediately over the stile go right to follow your original line, now with the hedge on your right, to the bottom corner. Here there is another step stile after which you walk 15 yards forward to cross a plank footbridge. Now with a hedge on your right walk forward and up to the top field corner where you cross a step stile into a very short section of enclosed path and so enter another field.

Diddlebury Delights 83

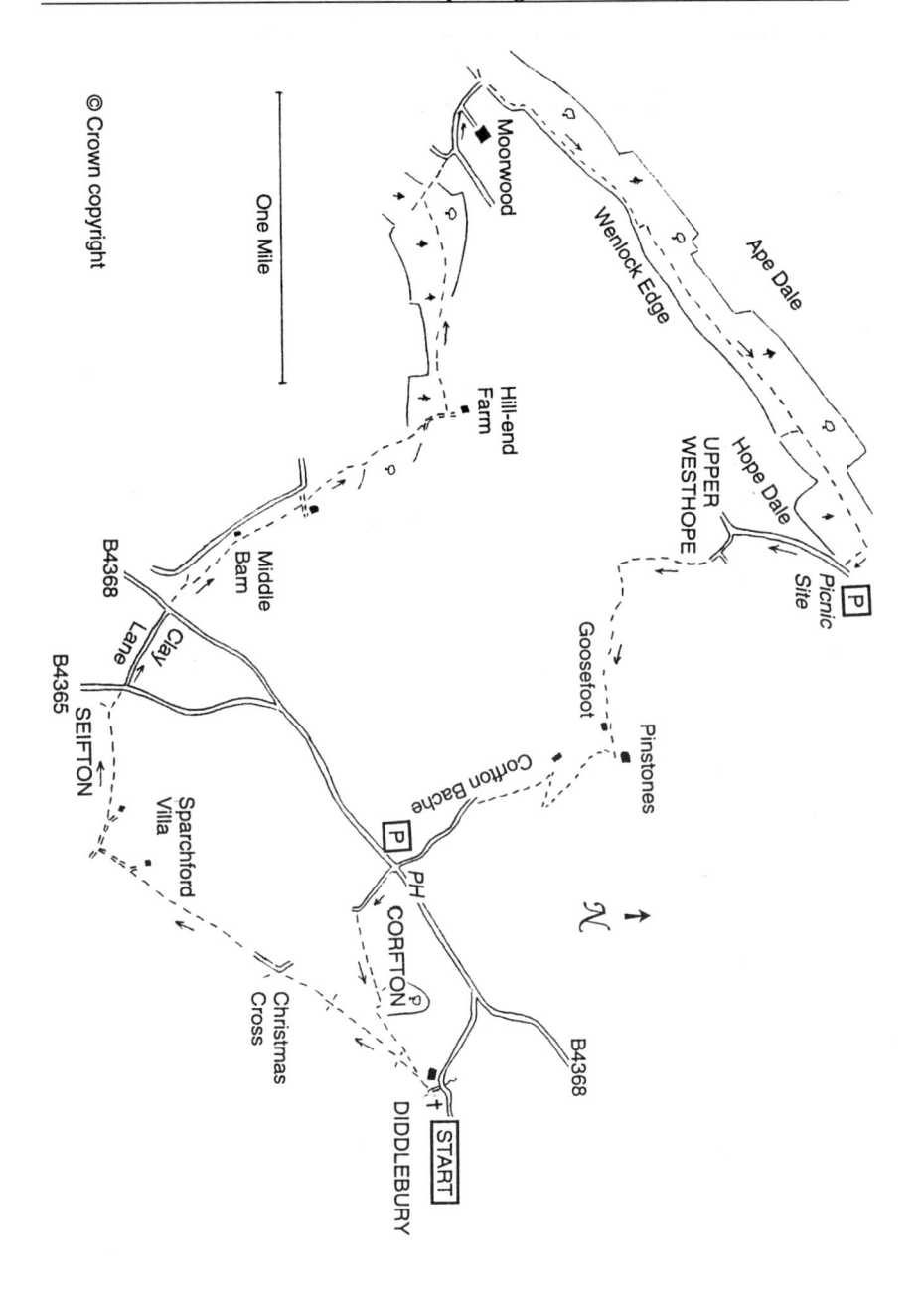

Just a few yards to your right is a step stile that takes you into a green lane. This is Christmas Cross.

Go left and follow the lane for the short distance where it spills into a field via a gate. Now following the right hand hedge continue the same line to pass through a gate into the next field and follow the same process to and through the next gate. Still with the right hedge now follow this third field edge to pass Sparchford Villa and so arrive at a gate onto the tarmac lane immediately before the entrance to the villa.

Turn left along the lane and follow it to a sharp left bend. On your right is a gateway with a public footpath sign. Go right through the gate and follow a track to the field corner left of a white cottage. In this corner there is a hedge gap and a waymark post where you leave the track to go through the gap into a field. In the field you are faced with a large field crossing where the way may not be trodden. Go forward across the field, slightly left, to cross it diagonally on a bearing of 280 degrees and, although you cannot yet see it, heading for the top farmost left corner. On the way you will pass a recessed square shape in the left boundary.

Arriving at your targeted corner you will see a waymarked step stile which you cross into a narrow field. Here walk across the field to a gate in the opposite hedge, just right of a house, and so join the B4365. Almost opposite is a T-junction which is Clay Lane. Now follow Clay Lane all the way to its junction with the B4368 where opposite is a sunken and signed bridleway.

Entering the bridleway – *notice the layered limestone formations typical of this area* – follow it the short way to a second gated stile. On the other side continue upwards, to your right you will see the sides of the attractive Seifton Batch, to reach two adjacent gated step stiles. Cross the right hand one and follow the obvious depression along the field edge with a hedge left – on the other side of the hedge is a parallel and surfaced farm road. With the field edge pass right of Middle Barn and continue with the hedge to the top field corner just before cottages. Go up and through the gap in the field corner to follow the hedge (left) and a fence (right) to meet the drive to the cottages.

Cross the drive to the signed hurdle gate opposite and pass through to continue forward and up into the original hedged bridleway. This shortly brings you to a hunter's gate and so into a field where you follow the bottom edge with a hedge and fence on your right. Quickly meeting a woodland corner continue along the bottom of the field now with the woodland on your right until arriving at the inverted field corner where there is a gate and metal water trough.

Pass through the gate and soon descend to merge with a tarmac track coming up from the right. Going forward with it as it swings right towards Hill-End Farm you will see a waymarked bridleway marker post up on

Diddlebury Delights 85

the left just before the converted 'Stone Barn'. Go left with the bridleway as it steeply climbs behind the farm buildings, at the edge of woodland. Arriving at a gate pass through, continuing forward and slightly down to merge with a track coming down from the left.

Follow the terraced track through another gate and follow the bottom edge of the woodland. Through another gate stay with the broad track, now through conifers, for some way until your track merges with another track coming down from the left. Follow it down to soon pass a footpath sign and then immediately arrive at a track junction. Here go forward and down on the broad forestry road – with a fence and fields (left) and woodland (right) – to soon arrive at a horizontal pole vehicle barrier. This takes you onto a surfaced lane at a bend.

Join the lane and go forward for 25 yards to its next bend and Y-junction. Here go left along the minor lane that bears an old and broken 'No Through Road' sign. Follow it to the point where the tarmac swings right towards 'Moorwood' and here on the bend leave it to continue forward along the hedged and roughly surfaced lane that shortly brings you to the top of Wenlock Edge.

Here, at the Forestry Commission sign 'Strefford Wood', you have quite stunning views forward and back. Turn right at the sign to now follow the wooded top of Wenlock Edge for the next two miles. On the way you will get occasional views left across Ape Dale to the Long Mynd, Caer Caradoc and The Lawley. To the right and across Hope Dale can be seen the tree clad whale back of Callow Hill with its rectangular hill-top tower.

After a little over 1½ miles you will come to a footpath marker post in Long Coppice. This indicates a path left and down the Edge, and one right out of the woodland – as well as yours straight ahead. Continue ahead for a further half mile until the track swings sharp right – this is almost at the end of the mature woodland. However, instead of turning right here, your way continues forward for another 50 yards to the end of the mature woodland and the start of a young plantation. Here follow the way right as it passes between the older and the younger trees to reach a narrow road. Here turn right to reach Harton Hollow car park and picnic area.

The picnic area is looked after by the Shropshire Conservation Trust and is the start of the Edge Wood Nature Trail.

Passing the picnic area continue along the road to the finger post at Upper Westhope where you turn left with the sign for 'Middlehope 2'. In a short way the tarmac lane you are following turns sharp left. Here you continue straight ahead up a secondary tarmac lane to pass through a gate and then right of cottages. As the drive goes left towards the cottages you walk to the gate in the corner and so enter a lovely green lane. Follow the grassy lane as it gently rises to the right hand edge of woodland and a gate. *Pause here to enjoy views that mere words cannot describe.*

Through the gate and up the track along the woodland edge will take you over a crossing track to then merge with a track coming up from the right. Continue forward through the trees, now on a short level stretch, to arrive at a gate through which you merge with another track coming up from the right. Forward again, leaving the woodland behind, to walk between hedgerows will bring you to a field corner and an obvious junction of bridleways. Here one goes right along the field edge and the other (yours) left through the gate.

Turn left through the gate and then immediately right to follow the right hand hedge through two more gates and so left of the curiously named 'Goosefoot' cottage. This will bring you to another gate into the edge of Pinstones farmyard. Here there is another gate immediately to your right which takes a drive down to 'Goosefoot'. Go right to this second gate and immediately through it go left with the fence to a low marker post. Now keeping the fence on your left follow it to walk above the delightful Corfton Bache which is to your right and below.

This is not the line of the Public Bridleway shown on the Pathfinder and Definitive maps which instead passes through the residence in the valley bottom. Rather you are following a permissive route known by the County Council as the 'Corvedale Recreational Route' and waymarked with low marker posts carrying white arrows.

Stay with the left hedge/fence until reaching a gate in it. Close to the gate is a marker post – both are in line with a telegraph pole and the last of the pools in the valley bottom – where a broad, grassy track goes acutely right (almost back on yourself) taking you down to another marker post in front of the gate to the residence. Here turn acutely left to join the bottom track and so follow it, away from the buildings, down the valley floor. In a little while the track becomes a hedged green lane and arrives at a gate. Through the gate, now onto tarmac, pass a cottage and then continue down the lane to pass more houses and so reach the Sun Inn on the B4368 at Corfton.

Following the 'No Through Road' opposite signed for Lower Corfton you will pass 'Lower House' where the road forks. Here go ahead (right) as far as 'Beechwood' where the road forks again. Go left through the metal kissing gate at the side of a white metal gate and quickly through another kissing gate into a field at the side of a drive.

In the field go forward and slightly left, east, to cut the corner of the field and arrive at a wooden gate in the hedge ahead. Go through the gate and immediately over the culverted stream to strike up the field, moving away from the left hand hedge, to go diagonally right to the far top right corner. Here there is a hunter's gate next to the hedge surrounding a young deciduous plantation. Through the hunter's gate follow the left hand hedge for 35 yards where there is another hunter's gate. Go left through this into the parkland pasture of your outward journey from Diddlebury.

Now, bearing very slightly right, cross the parkland (60 degrees) to the step stile in the opposite fence that you crossed earlier. From here just descend the sloping field back to the footbridge and the start.

Diddlebury church

17
Banners for the Buzzards
Craven Arms

Following its long recovery from that awful disease myxomatosis, the new immunity of the rabbit may not be welcomed by all. On this walk though you will likely see one species that positively welcomes the rabbit's return – the buzzard. As its main food source was decimated over the last thirty years, so the buzzard population declined. Today, with the return of the rabbit, buzzard numbers are increasing and the population is gradually spreading eastwards. For me, the buzzard's plaintive cry epitomizes the call of the wild.

In places, the walk connects with the Shropshire Way which is appropriately waymarked with a buzzard symbol. Taking in attractive countryside and some breathtaking views this walk may also be divided into two shorter excursions.

> DISTANCE: 14 miles, 7 miles, 7 miles.
> MAPS: Landranger (1:50,000) 137. Pathfinder (1:25,000) 930 & 931.
> PARKING: Public car park in Craven Arms. Limited road-side in Aston on Clun.
> PUBLIC TRANSPORT: British Rail to Craven Arms, *or* Midland Red West service 435 (Ludlow-Craven Arms-Shrewsbury).
> START/FINISH: Market Street, Craven Arms. GR 434828 *or* The Arbor Tree in Aston on Clun. GR 393817 (✳ on page 91).

FROM the B4368 in Craven Arms follow Market Street beyond the Stokesay Hotel to meet the A49(T). Cross over to Dodds Lane opposite and follow it to pass under a railway bridge and then arrive at a gate into a field. In the field and to your right you will see another railway line that you now follow forward, across the fields, to meet a road.

On the road – the Roman Watling Street – turn right to pass under the railway bridge and so arrive at the B4368. Here cross the B4368 and continue with the Roman road for a little under 200 yards where, just before a house, you will see a step stile right and a gate and fence stile left. Go over the left fence stile and walk slightly left across the field (285 degrees) to reach a gated step stile in the opposite hedge. Over this go forward with a hedge on your left and in the next corner cross another fence stile to continue forward, again with the hedge on your left. In a further 100 yards you will come to a waymarked gate, left, which you pass through. Now go diagonally right across the field heading for a gate gap (260 degrees) half way along the opposite fence. Through this, and in the

Banners for the Buzzards

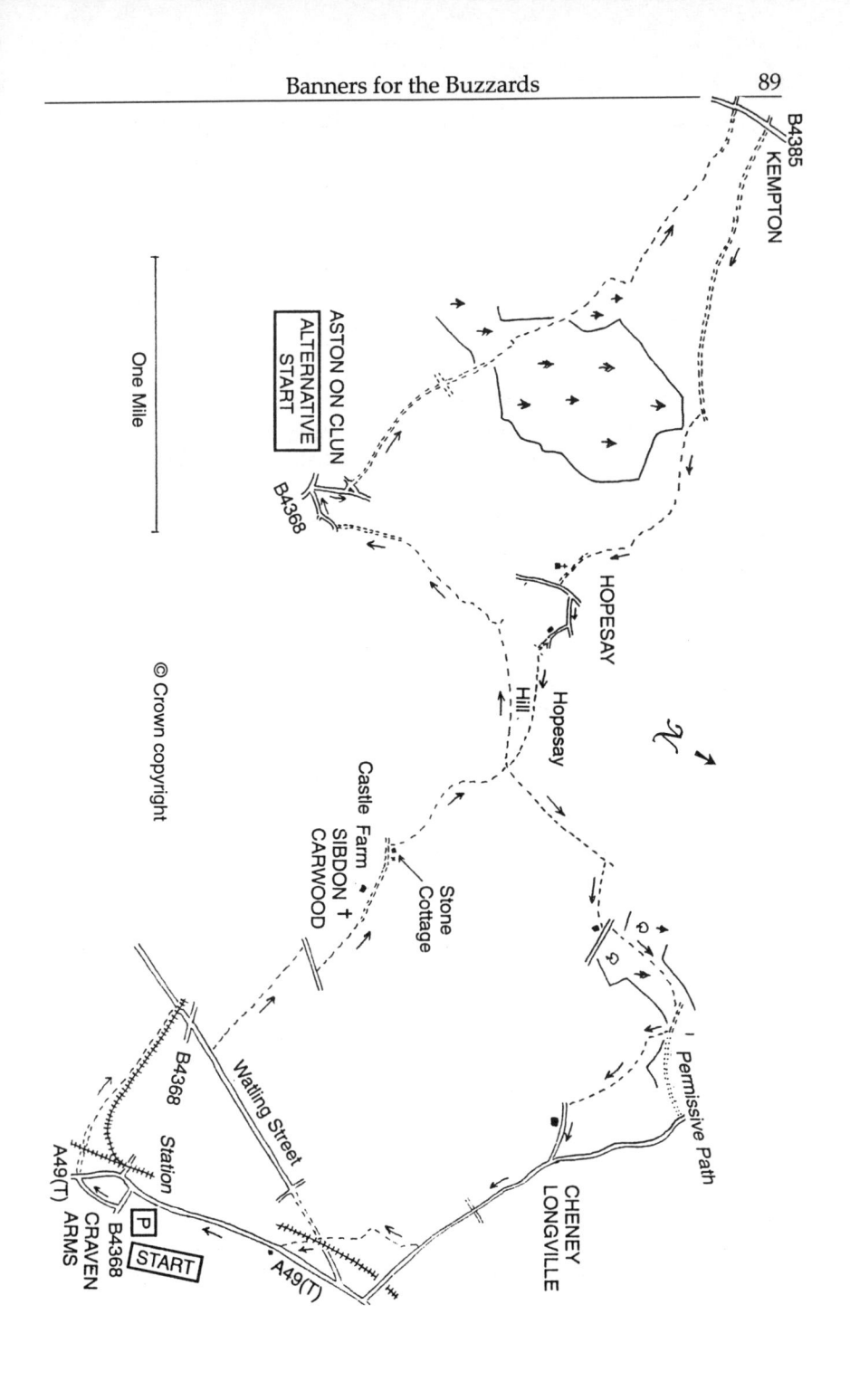

next field, go half right again (295 degrees) to a stile in the right hand hedge which is in front of a telegraph pole and right of a gate. Cross over onto a tarmac lane and turn right.

Follow the lane for approximately 200 yards where, on the right, you will see double gates and a cattle grid and, to the left, a step stile. Go left over the step stile and follow the right hand hedge up the field to a gate in the top corner. Through the gate continue forward along an unsurfaced track between stone walls, passing right of a large house and then between farm buildings, to a gate right of sheep pens and another house. Pass through the gate into a large field and go forward to merge with a track before arriving at a small stone cottage.

In front of the cottage leave the track by going left, just before a group of oak trees, to follow tyre tracks towards a shallow gully between trees.

Immediately after turning left in front of the cottage, and before the shallow gully, turn right to follow the garden boundary to a broad, waymarked, fence stile on the left side of the cottage. Cross over this and walk up a tree lined sunken track and continue rising, keeping the remains of a hedge on your right. Well before the top of the field veer slightly left, away from the hedge, so as to arrive at a gate in the top fence.

Through the gate walk up with the left fence into a large sloping field. Continue forward along the field edge, with the left woodland fence, to the far lower corner where you will see a ruined brick building. Here pass between the fence and the ruin to the gate just beyond. Go through the gate and still following the left fence and woodland arrive at a gate in the next corner that gives access onto the National Trust's Hopesay Hill Common. Go through onto the common.

For the shorter route back to Craven Arms turn right and follow the directions from ➤➤ *on page 93. For the longer route continue from the next paragraph.*

On the common go half left ➤ (on a general bearing of 240 degrees) to follow a grassy swathe over the rounded mound. As you start to descend, with wonderful views of the South Shropshire Hills, you will pass left of a clump of conifer trees. Quickly afterwards the track will take you through a gap in a line of stunted trees – the remains of a hedge. Continuing down in the direction of the very large house in the valley bottom you will come to the corner of the intake fence where there is a white, wooden wicket gate.

Go through the gate and ignore the metal kissing gate a few yards to the right. Instead go ahead, slightly left, down a wide path through trees to pass left of a cottage garden and so reach a step stile. Over the stile and on the tarmac go right for 10 yards to then turn left through a waymarked metal wicket gate.

Bearing a little right follow the edge of new plantings on a fairly clear path. This will bring you to a step stile and into a sloping field. Here go straight ahead across the field along the edge of a slight embankment and so reach a step stile at the bottom corner of woodland.

Cross the stile and follow the bottom edge of the woodland to the next corner where you continue forward along a field bottom with gorse bushes on your right. Just before the end of the gorse, where it starts to bear right towards a protruding fence corner, aim straight ahead to reach the bottom edge of another large gorse clump. Here your way becomes a distinct track forward. Now simply follow this lovely contouring track until reaching the edge of Aston on Clun where you go through a gate onto a tarmac lane. Here go right and follow the lane all the way to the Arbor Tree and the B4368.

Decorated with flags this gnarled and ancient tree bears an inscription that informs the reader:

> The Arbor Tree is the legendary sole survivor of those decorated by King Charles II to celebrate the restoration of the monarchy on 29 May 1660. The tree was dressed on Arbor Day 1786 for the marriage of Squire Marston of Oaker to Mary Carter of Sibdon who left money to ensure that it was dressed annually.

✱ *This is your alternative starting point.*

From the Arbor Tree turn right over the stream bridge along the road signed for 'Hesterworth ½, Hopesay 1½, Edgton 3¼'. In a little while (about 250 yards) and opposite 'Blair Atholl' you will see a footpath sign on the left. Turn left along the unsurfaced track behind a cottage to quickly meet a crossing track where you go right. Follow this hedged green lane to eventually meet a wooden hunter's gate and a crossing bridleway. Go through the gate and over the bridleway to cross the step stile in front and follow a sunken, hedged track. This will bring you to a step stile into woodland.

In the woodland continue on the sunken path to soon cross another step stile and continue forward and upwards now merged with a track coming in from the right. At the top of a crest you will come to a crossing forestry road where you turn left for 20 yards and then right to follow your original line down another track. Arriving at the edge of the woodland and a T-junction with an unsurfaced track, go right for almost 60 yards where a footpath sign directs you left and down to a double fence stile. Cross it into a field.

In the field strike out half right (300 degrees) to cross an unbridged stream and climb the opposite slope to a fence stile half way along its length. Over the stile continue your line up the bank to arrive in the topmost right corner next to trees where there is a gate to your right and a wooden hunter's gate left. Go through the right gate and down the edge of the woodland to the bottom of a shallow valley.

At the bottom there are two gates, a wooden one in front and a metal one to the left. Go left to and through the metal gate to then go right down the field edge next to the right fence surrounding a gully. Follow this fence through a second field and continue with the same line through a third and fourth to reach the B4385 at a road sign near Kempton.

Turn right along the B4385 and follow it for about 200 yards when you will come to a cross-roads just before a telephone kiosk. Here go right with the Shropshire Way symbol to follow a lane – initially surfaced – for a little over a mile to its highest point. Here, on the right, where the grass verge is a little wider, you will see a wooden hunter's gate. Go through and walk half left to cut the corner of the field and arrive in a corner with two gates. Pass through the first one (left) and walk forward with the right hand fence/hedge for two fields.

Exiting the second field into a fenced track turn right to the second of two gates. Pass through it and turn left – resuming your initial line – to walk down the sloping field (110 degrees) towards a group of oak trees. Here, in the bottom corner, you will meet a waymarked gate. Go through, forward and down with the left hand fence and hedge. At a corner swing right with the fence to then go through a gateway and so along a track to a gate into a hedged green lane. Follow the green lane all the way past the church to the T-junction in Hopesay.

The church's oak lych gate, dated 1892, has carved on one side 'This is God's acre' and on the other 'Be thou faithful unto death'. Next to the church is a Wildlife Meadow.

St. Mary's church probably dates from 1150 and contains a thirteenth century 'dug-out' parish chest – carved from a hollowed out tree trunk – that is possibly the oldest in Britain. The church also houses a small colony of bats, a much maligned and endangered species.

At the T-junction go left along the road and then right along the road signed 'Round Oak 1'. In a short distance turn right along a lane at a National Trust sign. Passing a large white house leave the tarmac on the bend to go forward and up the hedged green lane to the gate onto Hopesay Hill Common.

Through the gate bear slightly left for just a few yards and then strike right up an obvious narrow path through the bracken, leaving the intake fence behind you. As you rise (a general bearing of 55 degrees) you will pass well left of and below a stand of conifer trees. Cresting a saddle go straight ahead to the opposite fence and a gate at the left edge of woodland.

For the shorter route based on Aston on Clun, do not go through the gate but turn acutely right – almost back on yourself – and follow the directions from ➤ *on page 90 above. For the longer route back to Craven Arms continue from the next paragraph.*

Do not go through the gate but instead go left.

➤➤ Now follow the fence to the top of Hopesay Hill and then continue with it almost to the fence corner beyond. Just before the corner you will meet a wooden hunter's gate and step stile in the right fence and just ahead, in the corner itself, you will see a field gate and a National Trust sign.

Go right with the hunter's gate and step stile and in a pasture strike slightly left (65 degrees) along the line presented by two dead trees. This line will bring you to a stone cottage (Hammondsgreen) just to the left of which there is a field gate. Go through the gate and join the road.

On the road go left and up for 50 yards where you will see a waymarked step stile on the right. Cross over into a field – there is a steeply sloping ravine to your right – and walk forward to the trees opposite where there is a step stile in the fence. Enter the trees and follow the distinct path forward and down through the trees all the way to the valley bottom where you cross a step stile and a sleeper footbridge.

This path appears to be well walked for at the time of writing it was quite clear and free from undergrowth. It was on this path that I saw, not one – but four buzzards gliding on the thermals.

Over the footbridge the path swings right to travel parallel with the stream. In a little while it then brings you to a pool and another step stile that takes you onto an unsurfaced track. Here go right for almost 100 yards to a gate.

Through the gate and forward is waymarked as a Permissive Route (see sketch map) but this involves additional road walking and therefore is not described.

Immediately in front of the gate the right of way is waymarked right and across a stream. On the other side of the stream cross the step stile into a sloping field and go slightly right to walk across the slope and so reach a marker post near a nicely shaped oak. At the post bear left to pass immediately right of the oak tree and follow a terraced track that soon descends to meet another track and a hedge at a gate. Cross the step stile at the side of the gate and follow the track along the left hedge/fence. In a while this will bring you to a gated step stile into a green lane. Bearing left with the green lane follow it to meet a T-junction with the tarmac in Cheney Longville.

Turn right along the hamlet road and follow it beyond the houses to a cross-roads. Continue beyond the cross-roads for another 320 yards to a gate and public footpath sign on the right. Go right with the sign and in the field go diagonally left (140 degrees) to reach the far corner where there is a gated step stile that you cross into the next field.

Here again there is a waymarked Permissive Route, this time clockwise around the field edge, but the waymarked right of way is now described.

In the field go straight across the centre (190 degrees) aiming right of an oak tree. Meeting the opposite fence go left with it to the corner where there is a step stile. Cross the step stile – and the one a yard or two on the left next to a water trough – into a field across which you can see a railway line. Cross this field diagonally right (160 degrees) aiming about 60 yards right of the railway signal opposite. This line will bring you to a marker post and a step stile into a hedged green lane.

Cross the green lane to pass through the hedge gap opposite and walk the few yards to the stile in front of the railway line. Taking great care cross the railway line and in the field opposite go diagonally right to a gate onto the A49(T). On the main road go right and follow it for the half mile back to Craven Arms.

St. Mary's Church, Hopesay

18
Severn Leagues
Wolverley

This longer walk passes through each of the three counties explored in this book and further takes in another stretch of the ever popular River Severn. It can be either walked in its entirety as, if you like, a challenge walk; or it can be divided into stages to provide a series of linear walks. Either way it is a fitting finale.

DISTANCE: 21 miles
MAPS: Landranger (1:50,000) 138. Pathfinder (1:25,000) 932,933 & 953.
PARKING: Roadside in, or on the edge of, Wolverley. Car Park at Upper Arley (Pay &Display).
PUBLIC TRANSPORT: Midland Red West service 5/5A from Kidderminster. Alight at Wolverley Sebright First School. Walk forward to the B4189, turn right and follow it to the Lock Inn.
START/FINISH: Wolverley (GR 829793) or Upper Arley (GR 767802)

FROM the Lock Inn, Wolverley follow the towpath of the Staffordshire and Worcestershire Canal in a northerly direction. Just before the first bridge leave the towpath by taking a clear path left which brings you to a house 'The Old Forge' left of the bridge. Go left of the house and then bear left in front of a parking area to follow an enclosed path and then cross the bridge over the River Stour to a gated step stile.

Over the stile follow the left fence forward to enter Gloucester Coppice. Follow the clear path through the trees and on the other side emerge at the edge of a field. Go straight across the field heading for the protruding corner of a hedge. At the corner continue forward with the hedge and in about 35 yards meet a crossing track at a gate.

Turn right along the track and follow it to pass right of a large barn. In a little while the main track swings right, back towards Gloucester Coppice, but you keep straight ahead to follow a right-hand fence. Shortly your track becomes enclosed and leads you to a gated step stile. Over this into a field now follow the right fence, high above the River Stour, to its first corner. Leave the fence to go forward on a clear track that quickly swings right to descend and pass between a pool left and the fence right. This brings you to two gates, in very close succession, in front of Debdale Farm. Go through them both to pass immediately right of a large barn and well left of the farmhouse and stables to quickly merge with a broad unsurfaced drive that swings left. Ignoring the right turn to the bridge over the Stour stay with the broad drive and its accompanying telegraph poles to pass containers on the right. The next telegraph pole on the left bears a waymark arrow pointing left and up a bank.

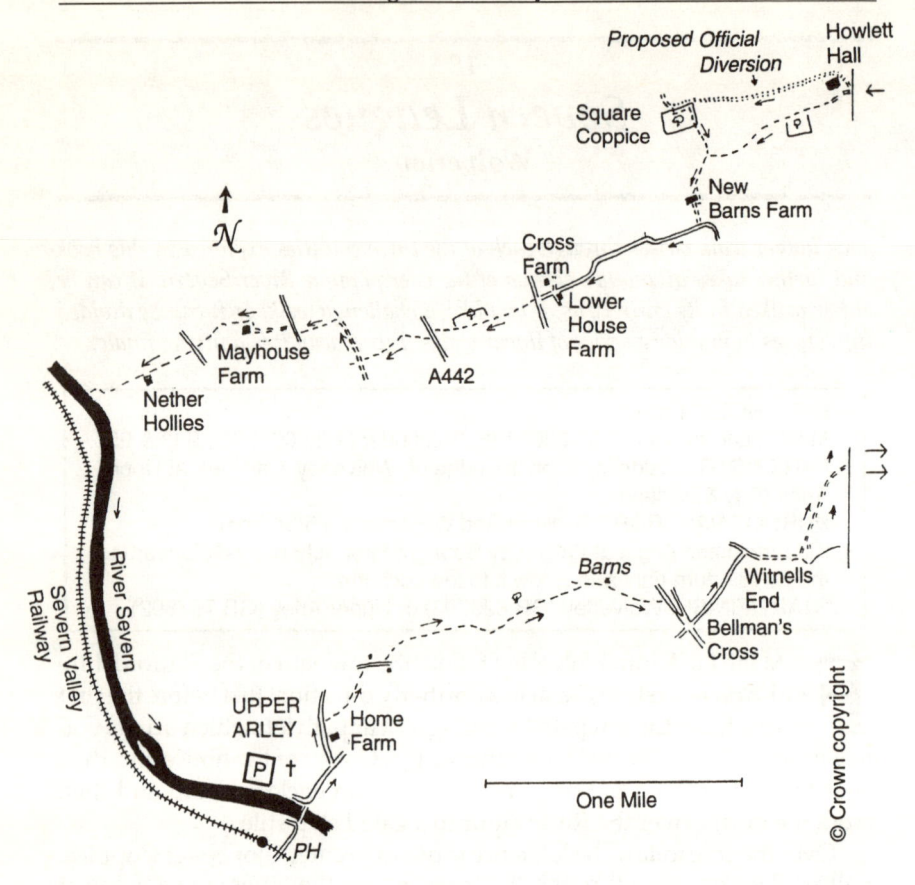

Go left up the bank to meet a step stile at the top and cross into a field. Walk directly forward with the left hedge to the next corner where another step stile takes you into another field. Maintain your line across this field, aiming right of a pollarded tree in the opposite hedge, to arrive at a step stile onto a narrow surfaced lane.

On the lane go left for 15 yards and then right along an enclosed bridleway. Follow this to its end at a road in Blakeshall. Cross the road, very slightly left, to follow the holly hedge for a few yards to a crossing track. Go right along the crossing track and follow it to a junction with a bridleway ahead and a footpath left. Pass through the barrier marked 'Horses' in front and follow the track for about 40 yards before bearing left with a waymarked path at another vehicle barrier. Maintaining the

Severn Leagues 97

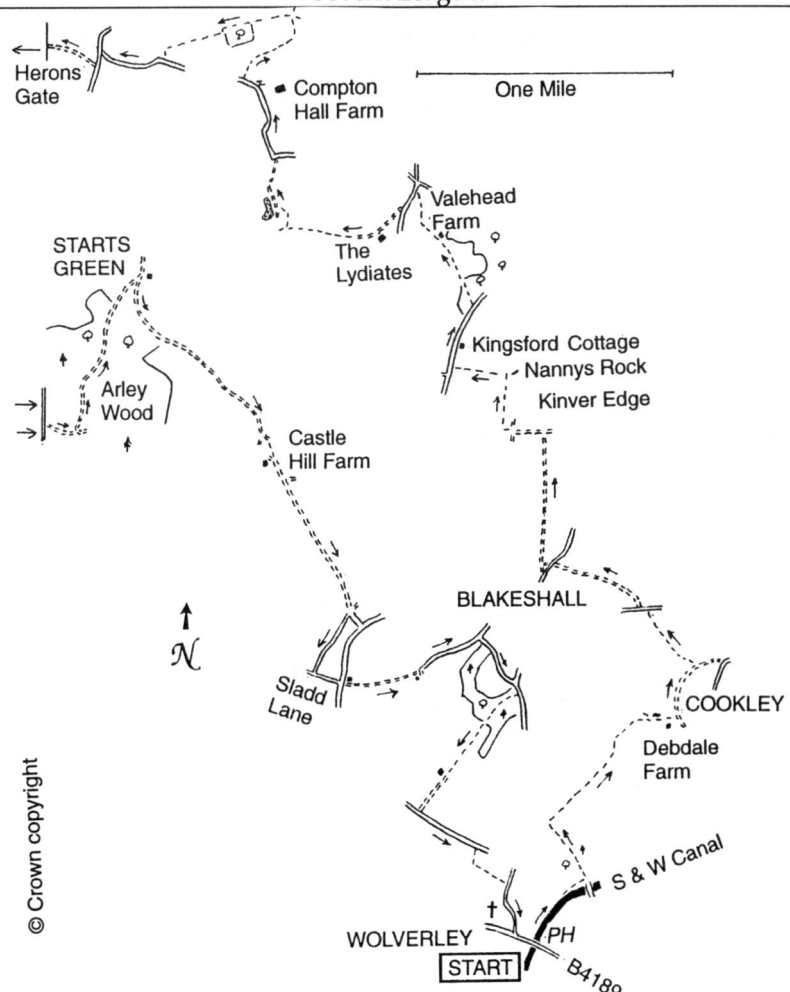

Map showing route with locations: Herons Gate, Compton Hall Farm, Valehead Farm, The Lydiates, Starts Green, Arley Wood, Kingsford Cottage, Nannys Rock, Kinver Edge, Castle Hill Farm, Blakeshall, Sladd Lane, Cookley, Debdale Farm, S & W Canal, Wolverley (START), B4189. © Crown copyright

same line along the tree lined path go through another double set of barriers, pass a bench seat and cross track and then join the signed North Worcestershire Path forward and up to another double vehicle barrier. Between the two barriers a blue arrow directs you left and up; follow it up to a notice board and sign marking the junction of three long distance paths on Kinver Edge.

At the signpost continue straight ahead and down the Edge on a stepped and waymarked bridleway. In a short while the main bridleway bends left whilst to the right there is a wooden vehicle barrier across a path. Go right through the barrier and follow the clear path as it contours to reach another wooden barrier, through which you immediately go left down a stepped path.

Just before descending the stepped path however it is worth walking the few yards forward from the barrier to the base of Nanny's Rock. This Bunter sandstone outcrop contains the remains of some of the rock houses for which Kinver Edge is renowned. Indeed further along the Edge two have been restored by the National Trust and are now occupied – as one.

While it is possible to get to the top of this huge rock, the path is something of a scramble and can be very slippery in damp weather, take care if you do. It does provide a dramatic view point: but watch your step for it is a sheer drop in front. The soft rock has been much carved by several generations of Kilroy!

To recommence your walk return to the wooden barrier and go down the stepped path.

Following the stepped path down, and ignoring side paths and tracks, descend continuously and reach another wooden vehicle barrier and a road.

At the road go right to soon pass Kingsford Cottage on the right. Shortly after this you will come to woodland on the left where a short distance ahead, on the left, you will see a public footpath sign. At the sign go left through the vehicle barrier and follow the clear path up through the trees where, after a little while, it swings right to follow the woodland edge and a fence down to a wooden kissing gate. Go through this and swing right to follow the right hedge/fence to the next corner where there is a step stile. Cross this and walk forward on a path through gorse to then follow the right fence all the way to a gate in front of 'superior' stables.

Go through the gate and swing left to the rear of the stables where a waymarked gap takes you into a field. Here cross the field to a kissing gate in the opposite hedge, next to a power pole. Through the gate and in the next field walk forward, across (350 degrees) and over a stile to a point in the left hedge just before the far left corner. At the hedge exit the field through conifers to the public footpath sign on the lane.

Turn left down the lane and shortly go right with the footpath sign along an unsurfaced farm road passing Lydiates Cottage and other houses to a farmyard. Here go right of the black barns towards the white farmhouse. To the right is a gate and white topped marker post with a sign 'Cross Gun Club – Caution Clay Pigeon Shooting in Progress – Sunday 9.30am to 12.30pm. Tuesday 7.00pm to 9.00pm'.

When shooting is in progress the club operates a marshalling system whereby a steward stops the shooting and you are safely escorted across the firing area.

Go through the gate and up the grassy track behind the farmhouse, shortly bearing right at a marker post, to follow the broad terraced track as it rises through trees. This will shortly bring you to a crossing track in front of a fence and step stile. Go over the stile into a large field, that you cross on a well trodden path, aiming for the pylon backed by trees – 280 degrees. Arriving in the corner by the pylon go down and cross a step stile to descend through the trees.

Just before the culverted stream at the gully bottom go over the step stile on the right. On the other side walk up the bank in front to the remains of a fence. Here go left to follow the fence poles to a fence stile that takes you onto an unsurfaced track at the edge of trees and near a pool. Go right along the track and follow it to a surfaced lane.

Turn left and follow the lane all the way to Compton Hall Farm. Just beyond the last farm buildings there is a signed step stile on the right. Cross it into a field and following the right hedge walk to the next corner and another step stile. In the next field follow the left hedge almost to the next corner and trees, where a double step stile and footbridge awaits you. Cross into another field and go right to the corner and then left to follow the remains of the right hedge up to another corner. Here go up the low bank and turn left to follow this field boundary and pass immediately right of a small stand of trees. *To your right you can see the slopes of the Sheepwalks (see Walk 2).* Beyond the trees maintain the same line with the left hedge to the next corner where you cross a step stile. In the next field do the same again to the next corner and another step stile. Over this go left for the short distance to the surfaced lane.

Follow the lane right until meeting the Y-junction at Herons Gate. Go left, signed Romsley and Alveley, and in about 65 yards turn right along an unsurfaced road – a signed bridleway – to Howlet Hall Farm.

At the time of writing Shropshire County Council have proposed an official diversion around Howlet Hall Farm which has been objected to and so results in a public inquiry. If, when you walk this section, the Public Inquiry has not yet taken place (or has taken place and the objection upheld) then follow the directions from ➤ *below.*

If however the inquiry finds in favour of the diversion then there will be special 'Official Diversion' waymark arrows in place and you should follow the boxed directions from ➤➤ *on page 100.*

➤ Just before the farmhouse the main farm road swings right, you however continue forward, now on a grassy track, to pass in front of the farmhouse. As this secondary track swings right into the farmyard you continue forward to a gate. Through this, immediately left, you will see a hedged/fenced track and next to it a gate into a field.

Entering the field go right to follow the right-hand hedge to the next corner accompanied part of the way by a wire fence. Pass right of a stand of trees to enter a field. Still with the hedge right – for this and another field – arrive at yet another stand of trees. Go through the corner gap right and turn immediately left to follow the field edge with the trees on your left. Arriving at the first corner (rounded) you will see, down on your left, a broken fence stile. Go down to cross it and descend to the bottom of the gully. To your right is a metal hunter's gate which you ignore and in front a small stream. *Now continue reading from ✱ below.*

➤➤ Just before the farm house the main track swings right. Follow it as it moves towards the rear of the house and then go right and left to pass immediately right of the far barn and so down to a double gate.

Through the gate continue forward along an unsurfaced farm road, that becomes variously fenced and hedged, and follow it for about two-thirds of a mile to the corner of Square Coppice where the road enters a field. Here (unless a hunter's gate has been put in at the corner) continue forward with the woodland fence for 100 yards to the rounded field corner where there is a hunter's gate on the left.

Go through the gate into the trees and turn immediately left to follow a path/track (back on yourself) along the woodland edge to the corner. Here the track swings right to follow the other edge and then beyond the trees continues as an enclosed track until reaching another hunter's gate. Go through this and in a few yards meet a stream in the gully.

Now continue from the next paragraph:

✱ Cross the stream and follow the right fence up the bank to enter a field. In the field go forward with the right hedge/fence towards the buildings of New Barns Farm. Meeting two gates in the corner go through the right-hand one into the farmyard. Walk forward for a few yards to turn left between barns then right to the front of the house. Here go left along the surfaced drive to meet a lane.

Turn right along the lane and follow it for just over half a mile to a minor cross-roads. Continue over, forward and up to soon reach a crossing road at a Y-junction. In the hedge opposite is a signposted step stile that takes you into a field. Here you have a very large field crossing. Walk forward across the centre of the field (250 degrees) passing right of a depression and, when you can see them, aiming for the left corner of woodland ahead. This line will eventually bring you to a step stile at the woodland corner. Cross it and in the next field follow the woodland edge to the next corner. Slightly left of the corner gate is another step stile over which you maintain the same line, following the right-hand hedge, to the A442.

Cross this busy road and follow it left for 15 yards to an oblique step stile. Entering a field go half right (290 degrees) aiming for a coppiced willow tree in the opposite hedge, left of the far right corner. Arriving here cross the ditch and a double step stile into another field. Now go forward with the right hedge, quickly followed by a right and left turn, to continue following the right hedge up to the top corner where there is a step stile into a hedged green lane.

Entering the green lane do not take the step stile opposite, instead go right and through a gate to follow the grassy enclosed track. In a while you will arrive at a gate across the track, go through and continue the short distance forward to where a pole fence crosses it. Go over the pole fence and turn immediately left to follow the left hedge/fence all the way to a gateway onto a surfaced lane.

Turn right for 50 yards and then left over the gated step stile. Follow the surfaced farm road to and through another gated step stile immediately followed by another where you then turn right just in front of a large barn. In a few yards you will come to yet another gated step stile that you cross into a field to turn left and follow the left fence. Stay with the fence all the way past the buildings and the old farm house – May House Farm. About 25 yards beyond the house pass a wooden wicket gate and continue forward with the fence to the next rounded corner of the field. Here there is a step stile left which you cross to follow the next field edge with the hedge/fence on your right. Just before the next corner there is a step stile right which you cross into the adjacent field. Turn left to follow the other side of the hedge/fence for the short distance to its protruding corner. At this corner strike forward across the field to a stile just right of a gate – and left of a house – that takes you onto a lane.

Cross the lane to the footpath sign and gate almost opposite. In the field follow the right hand hedge/fence as you begin your descent to the River Severn. Pass through a gate into a second field, near a pool, and quickly through another into a third field. Still following the right hand hedge/fence pass immediately right of the collapsed stone-built Nether Hollies to continue with the right hedge/fence steeply down to the riverside.

At the bank go left to follow the river downstream all the way to Upper Arley, some two miles distant.

On the way you will likely see kingfishers and herons. Though sightings are extremely rare, it is known that otters use this part of the river.

During this section you will pass large, scattered, rectangular shaped stone blocks. In the river's industrial heyday cut stone was loaded onto Severn trows (flat-bottomed boats peculiar to the River Severn) at this point and transported down river to Worcester where it went countrywide as building material. It is believed that some of this grit sandstone rock (high in silica) was used to build Worcester Cathedral. These blocks were simply discarded when the nearby quarry was abandoned!

On the opposite bank you will see a small, attractive cast iron footbridge that crosses a tributary stream and which bears the legend 'Coalbrookdale Company – 1828'

Upper Arley has a car park, pub, restaurant, a shop and a station on the Severn Valley Railway.

Staying on the east side of the river, near the footbridge go left with the road up and past the school to reach a road junction. Here go left with the sign for Alveley and Bridgnorth and follow the road past Home Farm and over a bridged stream. Just a few yards beyond the stream, on the right, is a public footpath sign, step stile and a gate. Go over and along the unsurfaced vehicle track. Just before the track descends to a gate, go left to the corner of a stand of trees. Walk forward and up, with a fence and trees on your right, to a gated step stile that takes you onto a roughly surfaced lane.

Turn right along the lane and follow it to the house on the right where to the left there is a signed step stile. Cross it, and another a few yards ahead into a field. Walk forward along the edge of the field with the right fence and trees. This will quickly bring you to another step stile on the right that you go over, to then cross a footbridge and another step stile, into a field.

Take your time in this field for it is easy to head off in the wrong direction!

From the field edge walk to a second gully just a few yards in front and then go left with it to its end. Here the right of way splits: yours is forward (very slightly right – 80 degrees) which takes you to a step stile at the end of a hedge and the start of a fence. Crossing over it walk forward with the left hand hedge to the next corner where you cross another step stile. In the next field continue forward to follow the left hand side of a line of trees – 100 degrees. This will bring you to a gated step stile into Nash Elm Wood.

A little further on the path follows a rather tortuous route through the woodlands so again take your time.

Over the stile go forward above a gully on a broad path and initially following the left hand fence. Soon it leaves the fence and rises to meet a crossing track where you go right and descend to a footbridge. Cross over the stream and walk 15 yards forward to a crossing track and immediately onto another footbridge where you re-cross the stream to your original bank. Now go immediately right up to trees – one of which is insubstantially waymarked – and follow the watercourse upstream for only a few yards when you will see yet another footbridge. Crossing to the other bank yet again now follow the clear path up through the trees to eventually meet a step stile that takes you into a field.

In the field walk forward with the left fence to its protruding corner and here continue forward and up (70 degrees) to a gate and step stile in the top right corner. Over this go half right, aiming for the right corner of double barns, and arrive at a gate next to them. Go through into another sloping field to walk forward and up, following the left hedge and quickly passing a tree and a water trough. In the top corner there is a gate and fence stile that you cross and in the next field go half left to the signed step stile onto the A442.

Behind you are dramatic views across the Severn Valley to the Clee Hills.

Go right along the road to reach the cross roads at Bellman's Cross. Here turn left along the road signed for Kinver and follow it for about a third of a mile to Witnells End where the road goes sharply left. Here you go right with the signed bridleway to pass right of a farm and then attractive new stables. Soon the unsurfaced farm road takes you into the edge of woodland where a marker post indicates a footpath right, steeply down a bank, and left the bridleway along the woodland edge.

Now follows some excellent woodland walking. This forestry, variously named Birch Wood, Coldridge Wood, Arley Wood and Castlehill Wood on the map, is in the care of the Forestry Commission and is collectively known as Shatterford Wood. Initially there is ample evidence of former quarrying.

You go left along the broad bridleway at the edge of the woodland. In a few yards the main track swings right to descend the bank but you continue forward past a waymarked wooden gate post. There are a plethora of paths and tracks in this woodland – as there are in most managed forests – but yours is quite clear and now continues forward close to the western edge of the woodland. In a while it begins a descent into a valley, now closely accompanied by over head cables that can be seen above you through the trees, to meet a stream and small weir.

Here the Definitive Map shows the bridleway going straight ahead, over the stream and up a bank. At the time of writing it was impassable however and the following Forestry Commission route is used to regain the bridleway.

At the stream and weir swing right to then quickly cross the culverted stream and so reach a forestry road at a hairpin bend.

Joining the forestry road take the left arm of the bend to rise with it and follow it as it bends left, in a while passing under the over head power cables – you are now back on the public bridleway. Staying with the road you will eventually arrive at a vehicle barrier and a Forestry Commission sign. Go through the vehicle barrier and follow the forestry road as it rises. In a little while you will see the white gate to a large house on the right. Here go acutely right to follow the enclosed bridleway that initially follows the garden perimeter.

This bridleway now follows a mini-ridge for the best part of a mile and affords lovely views on both sides.

Continue with the bridleway which after some way spills into a field just before Castle Hill Farm. Follow the field edge with a hedge left to meet a clump of trees and a divergence in the track. Signs point you left for the path along the left edge of the trees and a pool. In a few yards you come to another divergence where – ignoring the signed path to your left – you go straight ahead to the step stile and hunter's gate in front. Through this walk forward across the slope of the field to another stile and hunter's gate in front of the derelict Castle Hill Farm. Through this now continue forward and down an unsurfaced lane – ignore a left turn – and follow it for three-quarters of a mile to a junction and signs indicating Castle Hill Lane and Starts Green. Here turn right and follow a lane that passes right of a 'mobile' home park. Eventually you will arrive at a T-junction with Sladd Lane where you turn left – you are now on the Worcestershire Way.

In a short distance you will come to another junction where you go straight across, past Baxter Cottage, and through gates into a plant hire yard. Continue forward and up beyond the yard when you will see the remains of rock houses up on the left and also the evidence of underground caverns that housed factories during World War II. Your track soon becomes sunken and then reaches a fence stile at the side of a white house. Over this walk forward to join a road and then follow this forward to a T-junction.

At the junction go right and at the next junction right again. In about 30 yards you will meet a signed step stile on the right, just before a bungalow. Cross the stile into the trees and walk down to quickly cross another. Follow the clear track through the trees with a fence right. The end of the fence will take you into a field near a corner.

Straight ahead across the field you will see Solcum House. Head across the field directly for the left edge of the house and so reach a step stile in the opposite boundary of the field. Over the stile go forward with the right hand fence and through a gate to follow the same direction to the first of the house outbuildings. Just past this you will see a step stile in the right fence, opposite the ornamental gates into Solcum House. Cross onto the drive to go left and follow it all the way to Drakelow Lane.

Here go left and follow Drakelow Lane for a third of a mile when, with Wolverley High School left, you will see a step stile on the right set back from the road. Go over it, forward and down to the bottom left corner of the field where there is a white wicket gate and a step stile. Over the stile go forward with the left hedge towards the house. In the next corner cross another step stile to follow an enclosed path immediately left of the house. This will bring you to a road where you turn right into Wolverley village. Follow the road through the village to then meet the B4189 where a left turn will bring you back to the Lock Inn.

Index

Abraham's Valley	27	Coxgreen Farm	6	Hope Bowdler	70
Acton Scott Farm	75	Craven Arms	42, 88, 94	Hope Bowdler Hill	72
Acton Scott Historic Working Farm	74	Davenport House	67	Hopesay	92
Adams Hill	3	Debdale Farm	95	Hopesay Hill	93
Ape Dale	75, 85	Dick Slee's Cave	29	Hopesay Hill Common	90, 92
Arbor Tree	91	Diddlebury	82	Howlet Hall Farm	99
Arley Wood	103	Dingle Farm	48	Jacob sheep	15
Aston on Clun	91	Ditchford Bank	78	Jacob's Ladder	68
Banbury Stone	19	Domesday Book	13, 72	Kenelm	3
Barlaston	12	Downs Banks	11, 12	Kinver	37, 41
Batch, The	68	Dunsley	41	Kinver Edge	37, 96
Bellman's Cross	103	East Grove Farm	55	Knypersley Reservoir	30, 35
Berrow Hill	79	Edge Wood Nature Trail	85	Lawley Hill	72
Birch Wood	103	Enville	4	Little Merebrook Farm	57
Blakeshall	96	Enville Hall	4, 8	Little Witley	48
Bredon Hill	19, 76	Even Hill	17	Littleworth Farm	79
Bridge Farm	80	Fairy Glen	40	Lock Inn, Wolverley	95
Bridgnorth	13, 16, 64, 69	Forest Farm	78	Long Coppice	85
Brook Farm	80	Fox and Hounds, Lulsley	26	Long Mynd	72, 85
Brown Edge	30, 33, 34	Froghall Wharf	33	Longley Green	24
Brushmakers Arms, Barlaston	10	Gaerstone Farm	70	Lower Hartwell Farm	11
Caer Caradoc	72, 85	Gibraltar Rock	41	Lulsley	26
Calcot Farm	2	Glasshampton Monastery	51	Lutley	7
Caldecott Farm	54	Gloucester Coppice	95	Malvern Common	61
Caldon Canal	30, 33	Goodyears Farm	55	Malvern Hills	6, 19, 23, 57, 60, 76
Callow Hill	85	Great Comberton	17, 20	Marshes Hill	34
Castle Hill Farm	103	Great Comberton Church	17	May House Farm	101
Castlehill Wood	103	Gritstone Trail	35	Merebrook Farm	57
Cat Inn, Enville	4, 8	Hampstall Inn	53	Midland Motor Museum	66
Caunsall	39	Hanbury	76	Morfe Ridge	66
Cheney Longville	93	Hanbury Church	76	Mow Cop	35
Church of Saint Peter, Astley	52	Hanley Swan	57, 63	Nafford lock	20
Church of St. Anne, Brown Edge	34	Harton Hollow	85	Nanny's Rock	96
Church of St. Mary, Enville	8	Heakley Hall Farm	33	Nash Elm Wood	102
Clee Hills	6, 19, 26, 66, 69, 75, 103	Hermitage Cave	65	New Barns Farm	100
Coldridge Wood	103	Hermitage Hill	65	New Pool	61
Colwall	60	Hermitage Ridge	66	Newhouse Farm	7
Compton Hall Farm	99	Herons Gate	99	North Worcs Path	1, 3, 39, 96
Corfton Bache	86	High Rock	69	Norton Camp	46
Corve Dale	47	Hill-End Farm	84	Nutnell Pool	50, 55
Corvedale Recreational Route	86	Hoccum House	67	Onibury	45
Cotswold Hills	19	Hollyhead Inn, Bridgnorth	13	Onibury Tea Rooms	45
Coxgreen	6	Home Farm, Enville	6	Ox Hill Ridge	63
		Home Farm, Hanley Swan	63		
		Home Farm, Arley	102		

Ridges and Valleys III

Parkhall Farm	80	Shropshire Way	92	The Kettle Sings	60
Pinstones Farm	86	Shuttlefast Farm	59	The Lawley	85
Pixie Path, The	60	Solcum House	104	The Nelson, Longley Green	24
Potseething Spring	15	South Shropshire Hills	90	Tinster Wood	33
Quatford Castle	66	Square Coppice	100	Tom Holland Walk	62
Rag Batch	75	St. Mary's Church, Hopesay	92	Upper Arley	101
Ragleth Hill	72	St. Michael's Church, Little Witley	48	Upper Berrow Farm	79
Ravenshill Wood Nature Reserve	21	St.Kenelm's church	3	Upper Wyche	60
Red Earl's Dyke	60	Stable Farm	63	Valley Farm	78
Rindleford Mill	68	Staffs and Worcs Canal	39, 41, 95	Vernon Arms, Hanley	81
River Avon	20	Staffordshire Moorlands	35	Walton Farm	2
Onny	42	Staffordshire Way	7, 35, 39	Walton Hill	1
Severn	16, 64,101	Starts Green	104	Wenlock Edge	73, 74, 75, 85
Stour	39, 41, 95	Stepping Stones	29	Whittington Inn	40
Trent	30, 35	Stokesay Castle	44	Wild Edric	72
Worfe	67, 68	Stokesay Castle Hotel	42	Wild Edric's Way	72
Rose and Crown	50, 54	Stokesay Hotel	88	Witnells End	103
Seifton Batch	84	Stonehouse Farm	73	Wolverley	95, 104
Seven Springs	27, 29	Stretton Hills	74, 75	Woollas Hall	19
Severn Valley	66, 68, 69	Suckley Hills	23	Woollas Hall Farm	19
103		Sun Inn, Corfton	86	Worcestershire Way	23, 26, 39, 104
Severn Valley Railway	13, 101	Temple Pool	6	World War II underground factories	104
Shatterford Wood	103	The Hollybush, Brown Edge	34	Yelds Bank	72
Sheepwalks, The	6, 99				
Sherbrook Valley	29				
Shire Ditch	60				
Shrawley Brook	48, 55				
Shrawley Wood	54				

Some other titles by Trevor Antill

RIDGES AND VALLEYS: Walks in the Midlands
A selection of eighteen walks within the counties of Shropshire, Staffordshire and the old county of Worcestershire. Distances range from 3 to 10 miles, with a 'Challenge Walk' of 20 miles which can, however, easily be split into smaller sections.
ISBN 1 869922 15 8. £3.95. 96 pages. 12 b/w photographs. 19 maps. Paperback. A5.

RIDGES AND VALLEYS II: More Walks in the Midlands
Eighteen further walks, some of the areas explored being among the lesser known parts of the region. Distances range from 3½ to 12½ miles, with a longer 'leg-stretcher' of 17 miles.
ISBN 1-869922-20-4. £4.95. 112 pages. 21 b/w photographs. 19 maps. Paperback. A5.

THE NAVIGATION WAY: A Hundred Mile Towpath Walk,
by Peter Groves and Trevor Antill
Starting from the centre of Birmingham, the Navigation Way follows a meandering course through urban areas, rich in historical associations, and delightful countryside. It is described in twelve sections to provide a series of walks ranging from 5¼ to 11 miles. An additional ten 'canal-link' walks, from 3½ to 9 miles in length, provide some attractive walking in areas adjacent to the canals.
ISBN 1-869922-19-0. £4.95. 112 pages. 31 b/w photographs. 24 maps. Paperback. A5.
Prices correct June 1994.
Available from booksellers or direct from the publishers (*please add the following amounts for post and packing: order value up to £5.00, add 75p; above £5.00 add £1.00*).

Meridian Books, 40 Hadzor Road, Oldbury, Warley, West Midlands B68 9LA
Please send s.a.e. for our catalogue of books on walking and local history.